FAITH IN MARRIAGE

The Strength to Persevere, Overcome, and Thrive

DOUG BIERL

What others are saying about *Faith in Marriage*

"Faith in Marriage" is a real encouragement to take seriously the permanence and resilience of Christian marriage. Full of Scripture and real-life stories of God's grace, it is a fine addition to the many Christian resources currently available to those of us who want to strengthen and enrich our own marriage."

> ~ Dr. Russ Berg
> Crisis Marriage Counselor
> Author of *"Faith-based Discernment Counseling"*

If your goal is to explore the depth and mystery of marital intimacy that results in a vibrant relationship with your spouse and family, then I could not recommend any book more than "Faith in Marriage." Humility, authenticity and courage found in the person of Jesus and developed beautifully by Doug Bierl as it applies to marriage, is what you will find between the covers of this book. This is a read you will not regret!

> ~ Harvey Hook,
> Co-Founder, Convene Columbus
> Author of *"The Power of an Ordinary Life"*

"Faith in Marriage" is a compelling and carefully crafted book that captures critical Biblical Principles for creating a dynamic Covenant Marriage. Using his personal experiences coupled with the Word of God, Doug guides the reader from the valley of mediocrity to a "marriage made in heaven."

> ~ Diana Morgan, PhD
> Founder and President, Original Design International ®
> Author of *"Marriage by Design: Before Your Journey Begins"*

Thank you Doug for putting together these rich and simple truths for couples to benefit no matter where they might be in their marriage. "Faith in Marriage" dives into applicable and implementable scriptures and transparent stories to strengthen any marriage. I highly recommend this book to any couple that desires to take their individual walk with Jesus deeper and watch that transform their relationship deeper to experience the love and intimacy that God intended for marriage. Well done Doug!

~ Ford Taylor
Founder TL Transformational Leadership
Author *"Relactional Leadership"*

FAITH IN MARRIAGE
The Strength to Persevere, Overcome, and Thrive

*So then, just as you received Christ Jesus as Lord,
continue to live your lives in him, rooted and built up in
him, strengthened in the faith as you were taught, and
overflowing with thankfulness.*
-- The Apostle Paul (Col 2:6-7)

DOUG BIERL

ISBN: 978-1-7320425-3-7

Categories: Relationships
        Marriage
        Healthy Relationships
        Family Living
        Faith/Religion
        Christianity/Christian Life

Bible quotations used in this book are from two versions:

Cover Design by 3JPMedia

Dedication

To my children and their spouses, my grandchildren and their future spouses, and to all future generations, may this book show them why and how faith in Jesus is critical to their marriage. To all married couples, especially those who are discouraged in their marriage, may this book provide insight, encouragement, and hope for what's possible when faith in Jesus is at the center of their life and marriage.

Acknowledgements

This book would not have been possible without the love, support, partnership, insight, and watchful eyes of my wife, Julaine. I also acknowledge the many friends, mentors, speakers, and authors who have helped us on our journey, who have influenced our views on marriage, and who have shown us the importance of faith in our marriage. I thank God for sending Jesus as our savior and for making a way for us to have a relationship with God and, by faith, giving us the strength and ability to overcome every challenge we face.

CONTENTS

Introduction 1

Chapter 1: Basics of Faith 9

    The Bible as The Word of God 10

    Jesus as The Foundation... 13

    Our Identity in Christ 15

    Holy Spirit Is Inside Us To Guide Us 20

Chapter 2: Living Biblically Together in Marriage 23

    God's Design and Desire for Marriage............................... 24

    Biblical Guidance for Marriage 27

    Commitment in Marriage 36

    Love, Nourish, and Cherish Each Other 38

    Aligning With Each Other 45

    Investing in Your Marriage 51

Chapter 3: Praying Together in Marriage 53

    A Seed of Faith 54

    Models of Prayer from Jesus 56

    Six Layers of Prayer 60

    The Power of Two 64

    Rejoice, Praise, Give Thanks 71

    Praying Scripture for Specific Needs................................. 73

Chapter 4: Battling Together in Marriage............................... 81

    The Setting for Marriage 82

    Preparing for Battle 89

Battle Strategies in Marriage 96

Being Vigilant 103

Afterword 113

Appendices 117

Appendix 1: Enemy Arrows and Kingdom Weapons 118

Appendix 2: Overcoming Strongholds 121

Appendix 3: Breaking Unhealthy Vows and Agreements 125

Appendix 4: Recognizing and Handling Spirits at Work in Marriage 127

About The Author 131

INTRODUCTION

There is a reason you are reading this book. Maybe the title caught your attention and you are just curious about what faith has to do with marriage. Maybe you are in a good marriage, wondering if it could be better. Or, you're in a struggling marriage, not knowing whether it will survive or even not wanting to stay in it. Perhaps you are questioning marriage altogether. You are not alone!

It seems that more people than in any other time in history remain single longer or live together instead of, or before, marrying. Some people may be living together as a trial marriage so that they can simply move out if the situation gets too difficult; avoiding "divorce" by not getting married in the first place.

Why?

A driving reason might be that they no longer have confidence in the institution of marriage. Or, they no longer believe that marriage will last. Or, maybe they see no value in marrying, no reason to marry, or marriage as nothing more than a useless piece of paper.

It's no wonder that people have this perspective based on what many have experienced through divorce, or what they see

1

through family, friends, co-workers, or others who are struggling in their marriage. It doesn't have to be this way.

So, what is the key to a healthy marriage?

Jesus.

Jesus makes the difference. I'm not saying that there isn't more that a couple needs to do to cultivate a healthy marriage, such as communication and conflict resolution skills. There are many books written on those topics and others about various aspects of relationships. But, based on my experience, putting Jesus at the center of my life and marriage has made the difference. It undergirds everything else. If you don't share that perspective, then I invite you to read on with an open mind and make your own decision after finishing the book.

You may be saying to yourself, *Well, if Jesus is the key to a healthy marriage, then why do so many Christians get divorced?* Good question. The short answer is that things might not be as they appear to be.

There could be any number of reasons, but it's possible that one or both spouses believe in Jesus but are not living in the way that the Bible directs. Maybe they don't trust what the Bible says and so they make their own way through life without really integrating their faith. They might embrace Jesus in their head, but not their heart. Maybe they look the part of a "good" Christian on the outside, but they are hiding behaviors that go against what Jesus taught. It's possible that they aren't fighting the right battles or aren't using all that's available to them through Jesus to overcome challenges. Do any of these describe you? There's no need to be embarrassed if they do. I've been there too!

Can marriages last without Jesus?

Yes. There are certainly examples of marriages lasting a lifetime where a couple does not believe in Jesus, or their faith is not active nor expressed in their life. However, based on my personal experience, I believe that marriages have the potential of being so much stronger, healthier, and more fulfilling when faith in Jesus is central to the individuals and their marriage.

Faith in Marriage is about putting Jesus Christ at the center of life and marriage, which means that both the husband and wife have an active and growing relationship with Jesus. They live consistent with biblical principles. They pray together. And, they battle together for each other and for their marriage. This is what has made the difference in my life and marriage, as you will learn throughout this book. Over the course of 36 years through two marriages, I have experienced marriage without Jesus at the center and marriage with Jesus at the center. I know I wouldn't be married today without an active and growing faith in Jesus.

My Journey of Faith in Marriage.

Religion has always been a part of my life, although faith has not. Let me explain. I grew up Catholic, attended Catholic schools for 12 years, and went to church (Mass) pretty much every Sunday. I was married in the Catholic church and raised my children as Catholics, until I divorced after 15 years. Based on church doctrine, this meant that I couldn't partake in Communion, one of the central sacraments of Catholicism, so I felt less welcomed, although nobody ever said anything to me about my divorce. A year later, I met my current wife, Julaine, and we attended a Methodist church after we were married. Several years later we attended a Lutheran church for a year. About 10 years into our marriage, we switched to attending non-denominational Christian churches.

During the first 40 years of my life, faith was expressed though rituals or practices that were part of a Christian denomination. I did whatever was expected of people who were members. On the outside, I looked like the model man of faith. That was about where it stopped. It wasn't until Julaine and I were separated during our third anniversary due to my infidelity that I realized I really didn't have faith. More specifically, I didn't have a relationship with God and didn't know him. I certainly wasn't living out my faith.

This came to light during a business trip to New Jersey in early 2001 when I had dinner with a friend who was a former colleague. Julaine and I were separated at the time. After sharing a meal together and telling him all that was happening and where I was in life, he asked me a question. As I recall, he asked me if I "had accepted Jesus Christ as my personal Lord and Savior." I told him that I was raised Catholic and attended church regularly, so I thought I had.

He asked me the same question a second time. In that moment, the word "personal" jumped out at me and I realized that, although I had attended church regularly, I did not have a personal relationship with Jesus. I believed in Jesus and knew of him, but I didn't *know* him intimately. So, we prayed together and I repented and asked Jesus to forgive me for my past sins. I invited Jesus into my heart and received him as my Lord and Savior. In that moment, I really didn't know how life was going to change for me, but that was the beginning of my faith journey with Jesus.

Shortly after that meeting, I reconciled with Julaine, and a few months later, after several counseling sessions with our pastor, we were back together as a married couple and a family. It took much longer for me to regain her trust, but eventually I did.

After I began my faith journey, I read the Bible completely for the first time. I also read a constant stream of books from Christian authors about various aspects of faith (which was amazing because I didn't consider myself as much of a reader up to that point, except for business reading). Early on, I participated in The Walk to Emmaus, a Christian weekend spiritual retreat that was another pivotal point in opening my eyes to and strengthening my relationship with Jesus. Julaine attended the following month and it was a milestone in her faith journey as well.

As we were each growing in faith individually, we realized that we didn't bring faith into our marriage during the first three years. We didn't have a personal relationship with Jesus, nor was he a part of our marriage, even though we attended church regularly. It was the same during our first marriages, and we know now that the absence of an active faith in Jesus contributed to the disintegration of those marriages, as well as the early part of our marriage. So, we knew that for us to overcome life and relationship challenges, and for our marriage to succeed, we needed faith in Jesus to be at the center of our life and marriage. So, we chose to do that and have ever since.

I'd like to tell you that once I accepted Jesus as my Lord and Savior, everything instantly got better in life and our marriage. It didn't. My perspective changed, but I still needed to grow in my relationship with Jesus. As my heart drew closer to Jesus, I became a new man on the inside, which showed up outwardly. As Julaine drew closer to Jesus and we both put him at the center of our marriage, we grew closer together.

We now know that for our marriage to grow and thrive, each of us needs to be in right relationship with Jesus before we can be in right relationship with each other. Like human relationships that grow and change over time, our relationship with Jesus does the same. It always will. So, we continue to deepen our relationship through Bible study, books, church, fellowship with other Christians, and attending spiritual and marriage programs. We also started praying together, in addition to praying for each other during our individual prayer time. (It took us a while to get comfortable praying out loud with each other.) We engaged with individuals and couples who were further along in their journey and we connected with spiritual mentors.

All of these actions helped us have a more active faith and deeper relationship with Jesus and each other, and also gave us strength to navigate life and our marriage. While some of our challenges went away (mainly those related to behaviors inconsistent with our faith), we still encountered many. These included breaches in trust, discontent, job changes, issues with raising children and blending families, illness, death of an adult child, and many other things that were a part of our lives.

Early in our faith journey and marriage, issues and challenges were handled without involving God, but as our faith deepened, we approached them differently. We learned about our real battles and started fighting them together through the strength of our faith in Jesus. We've had our ups and downs (and still do), but we've found that when we keep our focus on Jesus and not each other or the challenges we are facing, we are able to get to a better place faster.

The illustration on the cover of this book is intended to artistically depict marriage with Jesus at the center. When a man and woman (blue and pink vines) have Jesus at the center of their life (vines wrapped around the tree trunk and main branches in shape of a cross) and they are deeply rooted with him (roots intertwined), and when they come together in marriage (gold wedding bands) with Jesus at the center of their marriage, it is healthy and strong (a flourishing tree).

We have learned three essentials to faith in marriage, with Jesus at the center – living together biblically, praying together, and battling together spiritually. In this book, I will unpack each of these and share how I've applied them in my life and marriage. I will be the first to admit that it's not the only way, but it's what I've learned and what's worked for me. Hopefully, it will for you as well.

My prayer for you is that this book will reveal new things to you that you can apply in your marriage, so that your marriage is all that God created it to be – healthy, thriving, and vibrant.

Chapter 1: Basics of Faith

In order for me to share my perspective about bringing faith into marriage with Jesus at the center, I first need to cover some basics.

This chapter is not intended to be an exhaustive review of the Christian faith. I am not qualified to do that, so I am simply going to share what's been foundational for my journey.

The best way to know and learn about Jesus and to have faith in him, is to study what was written about him in the Bible.

We read about what he did, what he said, what others learned from him, and how others were guided based on what he taught and what the Holy Spirit revealed to them. We also learn about how God wants us to live and relate to him and to each other.

The Bible as The Word of God

All Scripture is God-breathed and is useful for teaching, rebuking, correcting and training in righteousness, so that the servant of God may be thoroughly equipped for every good work.
-- The Apostle Paul (2 Timothy 3:16-17)

I have been a Christian all of my life, but faith has not been a focal point until the last two decades. One of the things I've grown to appreciate is the importance of the Bible to my life and marriage. I didn't read the entire Bible until I was 40 years old, so aside from what was preached at church, what was written in the Bible didn't even factor into my life. I am not a theologian nor ordained clergy, and I do not have a degree in biblical teaching. However, I have studied the Bible and have learned (and am still learning) to apply its principles to my life and marriage.

As the passage at the top of this page states, what's written in the Bible teaches, rebukes, corrects, trains, and equips me for life. Reading and studying the Bible helps me to hear from God, to know his will and desire for me, and to provide me with guidance, wisdom, peace, and comfort to navigate life's challenges. I now read the Bible to feel closer to God and to hear what he has to say to me. As a result, the Bible has become foundational to my life and marriage.

The Bible (aka Word of God, Scripture), is an ancient collection of writings, comprised of 66 separate books, written over approximately 1,600 years, by at least 40 distinct authors. (www.allaboutthejourney.org) It has been translated from the original Hebrew and Greek writings and there are many versions available. I will be sharing quotes ("verses") from the New International Version (NIV) of the Bible, unless otherwise indicated. Emphasis (typically in bold or underlined text) has been added to the verses to highlight words that are specific to the topic being covered.

If you are not familiar with how verses are cited, they show the name of the book in the Bible, followed by the chapter number, a colon (:), and then the verse numbers. For example, in the first verse quoted above, we see that it is from the 2nd book of Timothy (2 Timothy), chapter 3, verses 16 to 17. So, it is written as 2 Timothy 3:16-17.

As the verse at the beginning of this section states, all of what's in the Bible is "God-breathed" (inspired and directed by God). The Bible records what God wants us to know about him, Jesus, and the Holy Spirit. By faith, I believe it to be true. If you don't share that belief, as you read this book, I invite you to simply be open to the possibility that it is true. Ask God to reveal what he wants you to know and apply in your life and marriage. I will also share how my wife and I have applied the principles from the Bible to our marriage so that you can see how they are relevant, where it might not be apparent.

Here are some additional scripture verses that support why I rely on the Bible as what God wants me to know.

For everything that was written in the past was written to teach us, so that through the endurance taught in the Scriptures and the encouragement they provide we might have hope. (Romans 15:4)

For the word of God is alive and active. Sharper than any double-edged sword, it penetrates even to dividing soul and spirit, joints and marrow; it judges the thoughts and attitudes of the heart. (Hebrews 4:12)

So then faith comes by hearing, and hearing by the word of God. (Romans 10:17)

Throughout this book, you will see an abundance of quotes from the Bible that are relevant to the topic being covered. The scripture verses above provide the reason for this. God gave us the Bible to teach and equip us, to give us hope, and to speak to our hearts, penetrating to the core ("dividing soul and spirit"). Our faith comes from hearing and responding to what God inspired the authors to write, so it is more critical for you to hear from God through his Word than it is for you to hear what I have to say.

In order to live biblically, pray, and battle together effectively, it is critical to know what's written in the Bible. The scripture verses included in this book are an integral part of the message. Take care not to skip or gloss over them. Rather, let God's Word sink deeply into your spirit. By faith, trust that God is speaking to you and will guide you!

Jesus as The Foundation

---

*"Therefore everyone who hears these words of
mine and puts them into practice is like
a wise man who built his house on the rock."*
-- Jesus (Matthew 7:24)

In the verse above, Jesus tells us that if we want our life to be on a solid foundation, we are to listen to the words of Jesus and do as he instructs us. Luke, the author of the book of Acts, identifies Jesus as the cornerstone (Acts 4:11-12), which is a grounding point for a building. The Apostle Paul wrote "*For no one can lay any foundation other than the one already laid, which is Jesus Christ.*" (1 Corinthians 3:11) We are also told that "*Unless the Lord builds the house, the builders labor in vain.*" (Psalm 127:1a)

I am taking liberty applying this parable as a metaphor that can be related to marriage, even though it refers to our life (as the "house"). Jesus said that if we hear what he says (for us as recorded in the Bible) and put it into practice, our (marriage) house will be on solid footing. It will be rock solid. So, it's not just hearing and believing, but we must do what Jesus is telling us to do. Hearing, believing *and* doing are all required to have a solid foundation. Jesus also tells us that the rains (storms of life) will come, streams (difficulties) will rise, and winds will blow and beat (sometimes for a long time) against us and our marriage. But, when they do, if we are grounded in and walking out our faith in Jesus, we will withstand!

In my first marriage, even though we attended church regularly, neither my wife nor I had a foundation in Jesus, so our marriage house was not built on anything solid. My word to her was not solid. My commitment was not firm. My jobs changed, so we lived in many different places and had no roots in a community, let alone a community of believers. Our friends came and went. Our financial situation went up and down. Our emotional state and feelings towards each other oscillated, sometimes dramatically. We really had nothing to ground us when the storms of life hit, so our marriage house crumbled.

My second (current) marriage started much the same way, with no real grounding in Jesus, so the foundation was not stable and it crumbled within three years. However, as we individually and as a couple turned toward Jesus, grew in faith and relationship with him, and put him at the center of our marriage, the foundation of our marriage became solid and secure. Since then, when the storms of life have come against our marriage house, it has withstood the battering. It's not without damage, but the foundation is strong and the damages can be repaired.

If your marriage foundation is not built on Jesus, I urge you to adjust your life to put him at the center of your marriage so that you have the strength to stand firm when things come against your marriage that could otherwise blow it down.

Applying Faith in Your Marriage

What is your marriage foundation built upon?

If you are ready to put Jesus at the center of your life and marriage, as your foundation, what steps will you take to make that happen? What resources or people could help?

Our Identity in Christ

"Yet to all who did receive him [Jesus], to those who believed in his name, he gave the right to become children of God— children born not of natural descent, nor of human decision or a husband's will, but born of God."
-- The Apostle John (John 1:12-13)

If we accept Jesus as our foundation in life and marriage, when we invite him into our hearts, we take on a new identity. As the scripture verses above state, we become children of God. The Apostle Paul wrote, *Therefore, if anyone is in Christ, he is a new creation; old things have passed away; behold, all things have become new.* (2 Corinthians 5:17) Upon inviting Jesus into their heart, some people experience a radical change, while others may not feel or notice a change at first. In both cases, they have a new identity because they now have Jesus living in them in the form of the Holy Spirit (reviewed in the next section). They are "in Christ." They are one with him, because God says they are! By faith, they accept their identity in Christ.

Why is our identity in Christ important? For me, as I more completely embrace my identity in Christ, I live my life differently. The things which I used to do that were out of line with God's commands or desire for me as described in the Bible, have either gone away or occur less frequently now. Living by faith out of my identity in Christ has helped and continues to help tremendously when I face challenges that come up in life and marriage.

As both Julaine and I ground ourselves in our identity in Christ, we become more confident as individuals. We have less tension and conflict between us because we know that who we are is not based on what someone else says or does to us, but is based on who God says we are. When conflict arises, we are able to address it more quickly and we don't get as caught up in it as much as we did before. We still have our ups and downs, but we don't go down as far or stay down as long, so we recover more quickly. We are able to give more of ourselves to our marriage out of God's love for us.

The following verses from the New King James Version (NKJV) provide some perspective on what's associated with our identity in Christ.

Those Who Accept Jesus Are Saved

*"The word is near you, in your mouth and in your heart" (that is, the word of faith which we preach): that **if you confess with your mouth the Lord Jesus and believe in your heart that God has raised Him from the dead, you will be saved.** For with the heart one believes unto righteousness, and with the mouth confession is made unto salvation.* (Romans 10:8-10)

Have you invited Jesus into your heart?

If not, do it now. Ask Jesus to forgive your sins, tell him you want him to be your Lord and Savior, and tell him that you believe in your heart that God raised Jesus from the dead. Once you do, you are saved and you receive all that comes with your new identity in Christ, some of which follows here. If you are like me, you may not feel different right away or notice any difference, but as you accept your new identity by faith and deepen your relationship with Jesus, things will change for you.

We Are Promised Everlasting Life

[Jesus said] *Most assuredly, I say to you,* **he who hears My word and believes in Him who sent Me has everlasting life,** *and shall not come into judgment, but has passed from death into life.*
(John 5:24)

We Are One with Jesus and God the Father

[Jesus said] *I do not pray for these alone, but also* **for those who will believe in Me** *through their word; that* **they all may be one, as You, Father, are in Me, and I in You; that they also may be one in Us, that the world may believe that You sent Me.** *And the glory which You gave Me I have given them, that they may be one just as We are one: I in them, and You in Me; that they may be made perfect in one, and that the world may know that You have sent Me, and have loved them as You have loved Me.* (John 17:20-23)

We Are Children of God and Co-heirs with Jesus

The Spirit Himself bears witness with our spirit that we are children of God, and if children, then heirs—heirs of God and joint heirs with Christ, *if indeed we suffer with Him, that we may also be glorified together.* (Romans 8:16-17)

We Have His Spirit, The Same Power to Do Greater Works

But if the **Spirit of Him who raised Jesus from the dead dwells in you,** *He who raised Christ from the dead will also give life to your mortal bodies through His Spirit who dwells in you.* (Romans 8:11)

Now He who establishes us with you in Christ and has anointed us is God, who also has **sealed us and given us the Spirit in our hearts as a guarantee.** *(1 Corinthians 1:21-22)*

[Jesus said] *Most assuredly, I say to you, **he who believes in Me, the works that I do he will do also; and greater works than these he will do**, because I go to My Father.*
(John 14:12)

We Are Victorious Overcomers

[Jesus said] *These things I have spoken to you, that in Me you may have peace. In the world you will have tribulation; but **be of good cheer, I have overcome the world**.* (John 16:33)

*For this is the love of God, that we keep His commandments. And His commandments are not burdensome. For whatever is born of God overcomes the world. And **this is the victory that has overcome the world—our faith. Who is he who overcomes the world, but he who believes that Jesus is the Son of God?*** (1 John 5:3-5)

What all this means to me is that, as I take God at his word by faith, I am first and foremost, his son. I will spend eternity in his presence, starting now. I don't have to wait! I get to be in a personal relationship with him every day. I am one with God because I have the Holy Spirit in me, telling me what Jesus and God the Father want me to know. That gives me power and authority to navigate this world with confidence, knowing that I can overcome anything. It's not that I don't have trouble, but when I do and I stand on my identity in Christ, I am more at peace. I live from a position of strength.

For a more detailed review of the specific attributes of identity, consider reading *Who I Am in Christ* by Neil T. Anderson. He provides the biblical basis for how our identity in Christ makes us accepted, secure, and significant, which are three core desires that we all have.

Applying Faith in Your Marriage

As you read the statements associated with your identity in Christ, which ones are you having difficulty embracing? Pray and ask God to help you believe them to be true about you.

If you were able to fully embrace your identity in Christ as described, in what ways would your life and marriage be different?

Holy Spirit Is Inside Us To Guide Us

"And I will ask the Father, and he will give you another advocate to help you and be with you forever...he lives with you and will be in you."
-- Jesus (John 14:15,17)

Before dying on the cross to save us from our sins, as stated in the verses above, Jesus promised that God the Father would send the Holy Spirit to dwell inside all those who turn their lives over to Jesus. The Holy Spirit helps us to live out of our identity in Christ. The Holy Spirit reveals what the Father and Jesus want us to know. It's how God communicates with us! The Holy Spirit reveals truth to us, gives us wisdom, comfort, hope, peace, and counsel.

Jesus said:

*"If you love me, keep my commands. **And I will ask the Father, and he will give you another advocate to help you and be with you forever**— the Spirit of truth. The world cannot accept him, because it neither sees him nor knows him. But you know him, for **he lives with you and will be in you**.* (John 14:15-17)

But the Advocate [Comforter], the Holy Spirit, whom the Father will send in my name, will teach you all things and will remind you of everything I have said to you. *Peace I leave with you; my peace I give you. I do not give to you as the world gives. Do not let your hearts be troubled and do not be afraid.* (John 14:26-27)

*But when he, the Spirit of truth, comes, **he will guide you into all the truth**. He will not speak on his own; he will speak only what he hears, and he will tell you what is yet to come. He will glorify me because **it is from me that he will receive what he will make known to you**. All that belongs to the Father is mine. That is why I said the Spirit will receive from me what he will make known to you."* (John 16:13-15)

We are told that believers will experience life and express the fruit of the Holy Spirit.

***He who believes in Me**, as the Scripture has said, **out of his heart will flow rivers of living water**.* (John 7:38)

*But the **fruit of the Spirit is love, joy, peace, forbearance, kindness, goodness, faithfulness, gentleness and self-control**.* (Galatians 5:22-23)

So, when we are connecting with, listening to, and following Jesus as guided by the Holy Spirit, these things flow from us. Unfortunately, when we choose not to listen to and follow the Holy Spirit, we often experience the opposite, or at least things that are not very fulfilling.

It's taken me a long time to understand and embrace these truths, and to sense the move of the Holy Spirit in my life. It's still a work in process, but when I feel nudged about something that is consistent with the Bible, or someone speaks a truth over me that resonates deeply, or when something in the Bible hits home with me, I now know that the Holy Spirit is speaking to me. As I spend more time reading and reflecting on the Bible to draw closer to God, I become more attuned to how the Holy Spirit is guiding me.

Applying Faith in Your Marriage

What about the Holy Spirit being inside you do you find hard to accept? Pray and ask God to help you fully know and embrace all that the Holy Spirit is.

If you take God on his word in faith and receive all that the Holy Spirit does, how might that impact your life and marriage?

Chapter 2: Living Biblically Together in Marriage

The Bible is God's Word to us. God tells us about his nature and character, and how he wants to relate to us. He also tells us how to relate to each other.

A married couple that chooses to put Jesus at the center applies biblical principles to their life and marriage. I will share what I've gleaned out of the Bible to help couples do just that.

God's Design and Desire for Marriage

"So then, they are no longer two but one flesh.
Therefore what God has joined together,
let not man separate."
-- Jesus (Matthew 19:6)

Before we dive into biblical principles for marriage, it is important for us to look at God's original design and desire for marriage. Let's start from the beginning. After God created the world, he said, *"Let Us make man in Our image, according to Our likeness...So God created man in His own image; in the image of God He created him; male and female He created them. Then God blessed them, and God said to them, "Be fruitful and multiply; fill the earth and subdue it; have dominion over the fish of the sea, over the birds of the air, and over every living thing that moves on the earth."* (Genesis 1:26-28)

God also said, *"Therefore a man shall leave his father and mother and be joined to his wife, and they shall become one flesh."* (Genesis 2:24) This is God's original design for marriage. It is where marriage is first defined in the Bible and it shows the intent God had for a husband and wife to be joined together in oneness, physically and spiritually. Because man and woman are created in God's image, marriage is also an expression of God's glory. And, as stated in the verse at the top of this page, God's desire is for marriage to be lifelong. Marriage is intended to be an unbreakable covenant, similar to God's love for us.

So, how does the institution of marriage stack up to God's desire these days?

Marriage remains the foundation on which families, communities, and nations are built. I believe that's why God established it – for overall health and well-being of individuals, couples, and families so that communities and nations are strong and sustainable. However, in our never-ending attempt to control our lives and to take an easier path, the foundation has been crumbling. Even so, it may not be as bad as it appears.

"The vast majority of marriages last a lifetime; the current divorce rate has never been close to 50 percent – it is closer to 20 to 25 percent for first-time marriages and 31 percent for all marriages – and has been declining for years." (*The Good News About Marriage,* Shaunti Feldhahn)

Many marriages succeed today. The late former president George H. Bush was married to Barbara for 73 years until she passed away. John Glenn was also married 73 years to his wife, Annie. One of my uncles was married 68 years until his death parted him from my aunt. Every community has examples of long-lasting marriages. Our local newspaper publishes milestone wedding anniversaries on Sundays, and each week there are a handful listed. It is a paid announcement, so it is a small sampling of long-lasting marriages. If it included all marriages, the list would undoubtedly be much longer, and we would see that many marriages remain intact, giving hope to others.

Even when all hope seems lost, marriages can be saved. As you have already read, my marriage to Julaine is a resurrected marriage. We separated before our third anniversary after I walked out with no intention of coming back. But God wasn't finished with our marriage and he restored it. We have come across many other stories similar to ours where faith was a key factor in marriage restoration.

An active faith is one of the factors that strengthens marriage health. Weekly church attendance alone lowers divorce rate by up to 50%. Couples who pray together report having much healthier and more connected marriages than those who don't and "[When] both partners agree that "God is at the center of our marriage" they are twice as likely to be at the highest level of happiness in marriage" compared with those who don't share that type of faith commitment. Praying together also helps couples feel more connected with each other. (*The Good News About Marriage,* Shaunti Feldhahn)

I can attest to all of these things, which are now present in my marriage, but weren't always a part of it.

Applying Faith in Your Marriage

How does what was shared in this section affect your view of marriage in general?

How does it affect your view of *your* marriage?

Biblical Guidance for Marriage

Submit to one another out of
reverence for Christ.
-- The Apostle Paul (Ephesians 5:21)

The verse above provides the essence of the guidance given in the Bible about marriage. It is to be a mutually submissive relationship (focusing on the other person) out of reverence for Jesus, because of what He's done for us and the model he showed us. We are naturally selfish, so the only way that we can completely focus on our spouse is by the strength of Jesus through the Holy Spirit guiding us. The Bible addresses marriage specifically in the context of the relationship between a husband and wife. It also provides guidance more broadly about how they are to relate to each other when we consider "one another" or "each other" to be a husband and wife, and a "neighbor" to be a spouse. This section includes some of the scripture verses that I have found useful for guiding me in my marriage.

Married Couples

As noted in the last section, in Matthew 19:6 Jesus states that a husband and wife are intended to leave their father and mother and be united with each other, join together as one, and be married for a lifetime.

Even though the verse below speaks to husbands, I believe it applies to a married couple, which is encouraged to be considerate and respectful (aligned with each other) so prayers are not hindered.

*Husbands, in the same way **be considerate as you live with your wives, and treat them with respect** as the weaker partner and as heirs with you of the gracious gift of life, **so that nothing will hinder your prayers**.* (1 Peter 3:7)

A married couple is expected to fulfill each other sexually, except when they both agree to abstain for a period of time, always coming back together again so that they won't be tempted to look elsewhere.

*But since sexual immorality is occurring, each man should have sexual relations with his own wife, and each woman with her own husband. **The husband should fulfill his marital duty to his wife, and likewise the wife to her husband.** The wife does not have authority over her own body but yields it to her husband. In the same way, the husband does not have authority over his own body but yields it to his wife. **Do not deprive each other except perhaps by mutual consent and for a time**, so that you may devote yourselves to prayer. **Then come together again so that Satan will not tempt you because of your lack of self-control.*** (1 Corinthians 7:2-5)

A married couple is expected to be faithful to one another emotionally (in thoughts) and physically, keeping the marriage bed pure.

*"You have heard that it was said, 'You shall not commit adultery.' But I tell you that **anyone who looks at a woman lustfully has already committed adultery with her in his heart.*** (Matthew 5:27-28)

***Marriage should be honored by all, and the marriage bed kept pure**, for God will judge the adulterer and all the sexually immoral.* (Hebrews 13:4)

Jesus said that adultery is the only grounds for divorce, although divorce does not have to happen, if the spouse who was betrayed can forgive the spouse who was unfaithful, and that spouse commits to be faithful going forward.

I tell you that anyone who divorces his wife, except for sexual immorality, and marries another woman commits adultery. (Matthew 19:9)

A husband and wife sanctifiy each other (help each other grow stronger in faith), particularly if one of them does not believe in or have a relationship with Jesus.

For the unbelieving husband has been sanctified through his wife, and the unbelieving wife has been sanctified through her believing husband.
(1 Corinthians 7:14)

Husbands

In addition to being considerate and respectful to his wife as directed above (1 Peter 3:7), a husband is responsible for leading his wife and loving her as he loves himself and as Jesus loved the church, giving himself up for her. He is to feed (nurture) and care for (cherish) her, as he would his own body.

Husbands, love your wives, just as Christ loved the church...husbands ought to love their wives as their own bodies... they feed and care for their body, just as Christ does the church – for we are members of his body... love his wife as he loves himself. (Ephesians 5:25, 28,29, 33)

This means that a husband is to focus on the needs of his wife and place them over his own, when it is in the best interest of her and the marriage. When I care for Julaine consistently in this way, she feels loved and cherished.

Wives

What a wife is responsible for appears to be somewhat different from the husband, although I would argue that much of what applies to one is relevant to the other. Submission to each other and to Jesus seems to be a common theme.

> **Wives, submit yourselves to your own husbands as you do to the Lord.** (Ephesians 5:22)

To me, submission does not mean that as her husband, Julaine needs to do what I say. I don't force my will or myself on her and expect her to accept it. We have healthy dialogue and if we come to an impasse, she will often defer to me in submission. But I value her input and perspective, and I believe that God often speaks to me through her, helping to guide us both down the path he wants us to travel.

A wife is encouraged to focus on winning her husband through loving actions, and thoughts and attitudes reflecting her inner-beauty.

> *...if any of them do not believe the word,* **they may be won over without words by the behavior of their wives, when they see the purity and reverence of your lives**. *Your beauty should not come from outward adornment, such as elaborate hairstyles and the wearing of gold jewelry or fine clothes. Rather,* **it should be that of your inner self, the unfading beauty of a gentle and quiet spirit**, *which is of great worth in God's sight.* (1 Peter 3:1-4)

Finally, a wife is instructed to respect her husband, which is one of the core needs of a man.

...the wife must respect her husband. (Ephesians 5:33)

A Married Couple As "One Another"

The Bible provides many other ways a husband and wife are to live together when we consider how the Bible instructs us to treat "one another" or "each other" or "our neighbor."

A husband and wife are to love each other, have peace with one another, build each other up, and live in harmony with one another.

[Jesus said] *A new command I give you: **Love one another**. As I have loved you, so you must love one another.* (John 13:34)

[Jesus said] *Salt is good, but if it loses its saltiness, how can you make it salty again? Have salt among yourselves, and **be at peace with each other**.* (Mark 9:50)

*Let us therefore **make every effort to do what leads to peace and to mutual edification**.* (Romans 14:19)

***Live in harmony with one another**. Do not be proud, but be willing to associate with people of low position. Do not be conceited.* (Romans 12:16)

A husband and wife are to be devoted to and honor one another, humbly serve one another

***Be devoted to one another in love. Honor one another above yourselves**.* (Romans 12:10)

*You, my brothers and sisters, were called to be free. But do not use your freedom to indulge the flesh; rather, **serve one another humbly in love**.* (Galatians 5:13)

A husband and wife are to accept one another as Christ accepted them, eliminate division between each other, have equal concern for one another, and stop passing judgment on one another.

> ***Accept one another***, *then, just as Christ accepted you, in order to bring praise to God.* (Romans 15:7)

> *...so that **there should be no division in the body**, but that **its parts should have equal concern for each other**.* (1Corinthians 12:25)

> *Therefore let us **stop passing judgment on one another**. Instead, make up your mind not to put any stumbling block or obstacle in the way of a brother or sister.* (Romans 14:13)

A husband and wife are to set aside selfishness and put their spouse above themselves, encourage and build each other up. They should be pleasing to each other and serve each other without grumbling

> ***Do nothing out of selfish ambition** or vain conceit. Rather, **in humility value others above yourselves**...* (Philippians 2:3)

> *Therefore **encourage one another and build each other up**, just as in fact you are doing.*
> (1 Thessalonians 5:11)

> ***Offer hospitality to one another without grumbling**.* (1 Peter 4:9)

A husband and wife are to be humble, gentle, patient, sympathetic, and compassionate. They are to forgive each other, and carry each other's burdens, lifting each other up in love.

Be completely humble and gentle; be patient, bearing with one another in love. (Ephesians 4:2)

Finally, all of you, be like-minded, be sympathetic, love one another, be compassionate and humble. (1 Peter 3:8)

Be kind and compassionate to one another, forgiving each other, just as in Christ God forgave you. (Ephesians 4:32)

Bear with each other and forgive one another if any of you has a grievance against someone. Forgive as the Lord forgave you. (Colossians 3:13)

Carry each other's burdens, and in this way you will fulfill the law of Christ. (Galatians 6:2)

A husband and wife are instructed to speak truthfully and confess sins to each other. They are to pray for each other so that they may be healed.

Therefore each of you must put off falsehood and speak truthfully to your neighbor, for we are all members of one body. (Ephesians 4:25)

Therefore confess your sins to each other and pray for each other so that you may be healed. The prayer of a righteous person is powerful and effective. (James 5:16)

The Bible also cautions us about what *not* to do. A husband and wife should not lie to each other or become conceited. They should not grumble, provoke or envy each other, or talk bad about each other.

Do not lie to each other, since you have taken off your old self with its practices. (Colossians 3:9)

Let us not become conceited, provoking and envying each other. (Galatians 5:26)

Don't grumble against one another, brothers and sisters, or you will be judged. The Judge is standing at the door! (James 5:9)

A husband and wife are not to talk bad about each other, act against ("bite and devour") each other, or harm one another.

Brothers and sisters, do not slander one another. Anyone who speaks against a brother or sister or judges them speaks against the law and judges it. When you judge the law, you are not keeping it, but sitting in judgment on it. (James 4:11)

If you bite and devour each other, watch out or you will be destroyed by each other. (Galatians 5:15)

Love does no harm to a neighbor. Therefore love is the fulfillment of the law. (Romans 13:10)

As you consider all of what's written in this section, it may seem overwhelming and impossible to do. You are right in feeling that way! On our own, it is challenging to live up to all that's expected of us, but, by faith and through the power and strength of Jesus, we are able to love each other the way God desires. We may not get it right all of the time, but as we use these verses as a guide and as we embrace what they instruct us to do, we will have a healthier marriage.

Applying Faith in Your Marriage

What in this section challenged you about what is expected of you as a husband or wife?

What are you already doing well?

What specific areas could you improve to strengthen your marriage?

Commitment in Marriage

But let your "Yes" be "Yes," and your "No," "No,"
lest you fall into judgment.
-- James, brother of Jesus (James 5:12, NKJV)

The biblical guidance for marriage alone is not sufficient for marriage success. You heard me right. Biblical guidance alone is not enough because we have a choice as to whether to follow the guidance. Even deeper, we get to choose to be married. Aside from putting Jesus at the center of my life and marriage, a key difference in my marriage to Julaine between the first three years and the last eighteen has been a mindset shift around commitment.

Fully commit to one another

One of the most important things a couple can do to create a strong foundation for their marriage is to be fully committed to each other for life. Several years ago, I surveyed and interviewed couples who had been married a long time and asked them the secret to marriage success. I remember one husband who had been married for over 50 years at the time saying "when I said I do, I meant it." That pretty much sums up a common theme for other couples who have had long-lasting marriages. They fully commit to each other. Period.

Remove "divorce" from your vocabulary

A variant of being fully committed to each other is taking divorce off the table. Couples who love and commit to each other don't even think about divorce as an option. They are committed to working through their challenges and staying together. This was a key in my current marriage. After our separation, Julaine and I made a commitment to each other not to say, imply, or even joke about getting divorced. It's especially important in a second marriage since we both had survived divorce, which subconsciously could allow for the possibility of divorce again. That's likely a contributing reason why the divorce rate increases in second and subsequent marriages.

Doing these two things creates safety in the marriage relationship, creating an environment where it can thrive. Without complete commitment, one or both spouses will always be on the lookout for signs that the other is pulling back to be prepared for pulling out. It's not at all healthy for the marriage!

Applying Faith in Your Marriage

What is your level of commitment to your spouse?

If it is less than 100%, what is standing in the way and what steps can you take to be fully committed? (Note that commitment is your choice and has nothing to do with your spouse.)

Do you and your spouse need to remove "divorce" (or anything that implies it) from your vocabulary?

Love, Nourish, and Cherish Each Other

"Finally, all of you, be like-minded, be sympathetic,
love one another, be compassionate and humble."
-- The Apostle Peter, (1 Peter 3:8)

What would your marriage be like if you followed the direction given by Peter in the passage above? At its core, a husband and wife are responsible for loving, nourishing, and cherishing each other. (See Ephesians 5:22-33, NKJV) They pretty much embody the biblical guidelines for marriage shared earlier. When they focus on these three things *without expecting anything in return*, the marriage is more likely to be (or become) healthy and well. I am still a work-in-process in these areas, but when I do them well, we both feel more connected and better about our relationship.

Let's look at each of the three separately from a general and biblical perspective.

Love

In the Merriam-Webster dictionary, the definition of love is:
- ❖ to feel great affection for [someone]
- ❖ to feel sexual or romantic love for [someone]
- ❖ to like or desire [someone or something] very much
- ❖ to take great pleasure in [someone or something]

The Bible describes love in this way:
Love is patient, love is kind. It does not envy, it does not boast, it is not proud. It does not dishonor others, it is not self-seeking, it is not easily angered, it keeps no record of wrongs. Love does

not delight in evil but rejoices with the truth. It always protects, always trusts, always hopes, always perseveres. Love never fails. (1 Corinthians 13:4-8)

So, love is about being committed, patient, kind, quiet, selfless, putting up with a lot, and wanting the best for your spouse.

Even though this Scripture is read at many weddings, when we examine it closely, we will realize how difficult these words are to live up to. On our own strength it is, but when we turn to Jesus for strength, we have a shot at getting closer to this ideal. At its core, love is about setting aside our self-centeredness and focusing on our spouse. When we do that, we are more likely to be kind, to protect, to trust, to hope, to persevere, and less likely to get angry, to boast, to dishonor, to keep record of wrongs, or to fail.

Nourish

In the Merriam-Webster dictionary, the definition of nourish is:

❖ to provide [someone or something] with food and other things that are needed to live, be healthy, etc.
❖ to cause [someone or something] to develop or grow stronger

Biblically, nourishing is about edifying, building someone else up.

Do not let any unwholesome talk come out of your mouths, but only what is helpful for building others up according to their needs, that it may benefit those who listen. (Ephesians 4:29)

So, in the context of marriage, nourishing is about helping your spouse to grow from your support and encouragement through words and actions. It is about creating an atmosphere of trust and safety so that your spouse has the freedom to try new and different things that will make him or her stronger physically, emotionally, relationally, spiritually, professionally, and personally. This could mean freeing up time for your spouse by doing chores or other tasks that he or she might otherwise do. It could mean providing your spouse with notes of encouragement or connecting him or her with people and resources that can help your spouse achieve a goal. These are just a sampling of the myriad of ways that spouses can nourish each other.

One way that Julaine has nourished me in our marriage is by providing me notes of encouragement from time to time. Another way she nourishes me is by giving me books or articles that are relevant to something I am going through or a subject I am exploring. One way I nourish her is by doing things around the house to free up time for her to do things she enjoys. For example, times when she's especially busy, I will clean the entire house instead of just doing my normal share (cleaning the bathrooms). From time to time, I purchase roses or tulips for her because I know she loves them and it brightens her day.

Cherish

In the Merriam-Webster dictionary, the definition of cherish is:

- ❖ to feel or show great love for (someone or something)
- ❖ to remember or hold (an idea, belief, person, etc.) in a deeply felt way

The main reference to cherishing in marriage in the Bible is when Paul writes about the responsibilities of husbands and wives, stating *"For no one ever hated his own flesh, but nourishes and cherishes it."* (Ephesians 5:29, NKJV) This implies that we are to cherish our spouse as we would our own body.

So, what does that look like? A few years ago, Julaine shared with me that sometimes she didn't feel cherished by me. At that time, I didn't even know what the word meant, much less how to treat her in a way that she felt cherished. I knew it had something to do with being appreciated, but that's about it. A few weeks later, she came across a book by Gary Thomas called *Cherish*. No kidding. She found the book that addressed the question I had. He claims that cherish is "The one word that changes everything for your marriage" and that "By pursuing cherish, we become better lovers as well." He uses the book of Song of Solomon (also known as Song of Songs) from the Bible to illustrate how a husband and wife cherish each other.

Julaine and I both read *Cherish* and it went a long way to shift our perspective about how we treat each other. I won't try to capture all of what's in the book, but I will share a few of the concepts that have the most meaning for me. First, cherishing is about accepting Julaine as the only woman for me and lifting her up, especially in front of other people. It's about embracing her as God's perfect provision for me, paying attention to her needs, and giving her my full attention. In fact, when she interrupts me, I will sometimes ask her if she can wait a few minutes for me to get to a good stopping place so that I can focus on her. That little step has made a big difference in her feeling cherished.

Another way of helping Julaine feel cherished is how I respond to her in words, tone, and body language, especially when we are discussing a topic that is sensitive or where we disagree. My tone and body language can get me into trouble, if I don't pay attention. When I keep them in check and listen to Julaine completely, she feels more cherished. The same goes for when I am cheering her on and encouraging her with something that is important to her, rather than not commenting or perhaps even downplaying its significance. It's even better if I can help her accomplish her goal. Also, when one of us makes a mistake, giving the other the benefit of the doubt and extending grace is another way we cherish each other.

Another thing I learned from the book is that when I ask for her support or help with something I'm working on, it makes her feel wanted, needed – cherished. I recently asked Julaine to pray over me (which I don't do often enough) as I was preparing for a meeting. I think the cherishing bells and whistles went off big time! It didn't seem like a big deal, but it did wonders for our connection.

The book also helped me to be aware of things that I can do to make it easier to be cherished. I can change my appearance, behaviors, or habits that make it difficult for Julaine to cherish me. I also place her opinion of me and any situation that involves us above anyone else's opinion. I can allow her to love me or to help me, instead of exerting my independence. I can also be looking for ways to help her and meet needs she has.

The bottom line is that when I keep my eyes, thoughts, and actions focused on Julaine and what she needs from me, she feels more cherished.

Physical Intimacy

Physical intimacy is one aspect of spouses loving, nourishing, and cherishing each other. Caring for each other sexually, and meeting mutual needs for physical intimacy, is an important part of a healthy marriage, and it is God's desire. After all, he created sexual intercourse and it is the ultimate form of intimacy when it is handled with care.

For us to be physically intimate with our spouse, it is important that we feel connected with each other outside of the bedroom. All that I've shared about loving, nourishing, and cherishing comes into play. In addition, we've learned 5 "Ts" that help build and maintain intimacy – Time, Togetherness, Talk, Tenderness, and Touch. For us, participating in Christian programs together, studying aspects of faith together, attending social activities together, and doing projects together have also helped us feel connected. When we feel more connected, physical intimacy occurs more naturally and more often.

There's no magic formula. The key is to intentionally spend time together to connect with each other in non-sexual ways so that sex comes more naturally and is more fulfilling for both husband and wife. If you are faced with challenges with sexual intimacy, pray to God about it. We've found it helpful to pray before sex and also to ask God to "bless our marriage bed" as part of our prayer together. We've prayed this, by faith, and have been pleased with God's response! He cares about the sexual relationship between a husband and wife.

It may be uncomfortable for you to pray to God about sex. It was for us at first, but when we understood the perspective that a healthy sexual relationship brings glory to God, we decided to do it. So, give it a try and see what happens! If you don't see improvement at first, keep praying and eventually you'll likely experience a new level of physical intimacy.

Applying Faith in Your Marriage

As you were reading this section, what resonated with you?

What challenged you?

In what ways can you be a more loving, nourishing, and cherishing spouse?

What adjustments would you like to make with physical intimacy and how will you approach your spouse about them?

Aligning With Each Other

"If a house is divided against itself, that house cannot stand."
-- Jesus (Mark 3:25)

God's plan for marriage is oneness. One with God and one with each other. Satan's goal is to divide. He wants to separate us from God and our spouse (and family). So, the key to overcoming division is being intentional about aligning with each other. That doesn't mean that a husband and wife always agree with each other or never have conflict. It means that when disagreements and conflict occur, they are addressed and dealt with quickly.

Someone once asked me what I thought was the biggest contributor to divorce. I said that in most cases it all boils down to selfishness. When a husband or wife focuses almost exclusively on having his or her needs met, it gets in the way of the relationship goal of "two becoming one." Jesus said *"Greater love has no one than this: to lay down one's life for one's friends."* (John 15:33) Isn't our spouse intended to be our closest friend? While we may not literally give up our life for our spouse as Jesus did for us, we will need to die to certain aspects of our self-centeredness as a way of expressing love for our spouse. The Bible provides some guidance on how to be one and align with each other.

Remove all variance in thoughts, words, and actions

Variance is disagreement, or any time when a husband and wife are at odds with each other, whether in words, actions, or thoughts (ouch!). When this happens, it interferes with the Holy

Spirit flowing in each person and between the husband and wife, so it breaks their unity. God includes variance (disagreement) and strife (overt conflict) among a list of what we would consider more serious offenses. Paul wrote:

> *This I say then, Walk in the Spirit, and ye shall not fulfil the lust of the flesh. For the flesh lusteth against the Spirit, and the Spirit against the flesh: and these are contrary the one to the other: so that ye cannot do the things that ye would. But if ye be led of the Spirit, ye are not under the law.*
>
> ***Now the works of the flesh are manifest, which are these****; Adultery, fornication, uncleanness, lasciviousness, idolatry, witchcraft, hatred, **variance**, emulations, wrath, **strife**, seditions, heresies, envyings, murders, drunkenness, revellings, and such like: of the which I tell you before, as I have also told you in time past, that they which do such things shall not inherit the kingdom of God.* (Galatians 5:16-21, Authorized King James Version)

So, when we are satisfying the desires of the flesh, including variance and strife, the Spirit cannot flow, causing misalignment with God and with each other. We know the Spirit is flowing when we exhibit or experience love, joy, peace, patience, gentleness, and goodness, among other things. (See Galatians 5:22-26) When these are present in the marriage, it's a sign that the husband and wife are in alignment.

Carefully Choose Words

You probably grew up hearing or saying the phrase "sticks and stones may break my bones, but words will never hurt me." What a big fat lie! Our words *can* hurt. Alternatively, they can build up, producing life.

With the tongue we praise our Lord and Father, and with it we curse human beings, who have been made in God's likeness. Out of the same mouth come praise and cursing. My brothers and sisters, this should not be. (James 3:9,10)

What we choose to say is critical in all relationships, but even more so in marriage. If a husband and/or wife uses words that are hurtful, it causes division and breaks alignment. If not addressed, it can lead to resentment, bitterness, and ultimately contempt, which is a relationship killer. In fact, after years of research, Dr. John Gottman concluded that contempt is the most destructive negative behavior in relationships and the number one predictor of divorce. (www.gottman.com blog *The Four Horsemen Contempt*, May 13, 2013)

The Bible instructs us to avoid deceitful speech (1 Peter 3:10) and unwholesome talk (Ephesians 4:29). Proverbs 15:1 gives wisdom about speaking gently instead of harshly, and Paul encourages us to have conversations full of grace (Colossians 4:6). There are many more Bible verses about how we are to use our words, but the bottom line is that we are to speak in a loving way as often as possible. When I am kinder and gentler in my words to Julaine, we feel more connected than when I am abrupt or speak negatively, harshly, or critically.

Control Your Thoughts

Similar to words, thoughts can either build up or damage the marriage relationship. They can take a couple out of alignment with each other. Jesus said that thoughts reveal our heart, and thoughts of anger and lust are just as hurtful as actions.

*But the things that come out of a person's mouth come from the heart, and these defile them. **For out of the heart come*** *evil thoughts—murder, adultery, sexual immorality, theft, false testimony, slander. These are what defile a person; but eating with unwashed hands does not defile them.* (Matthew 15:18-20)

*You have heard that it was said to the people long ago, 'You shall not murder, and anyone who murders will be subject to judgment.' But I tell you that **anyone who is angry with a brother or sister will be subject to judgment**.* (Matthew 5:21-22)

*You have heard that it was said, 'You shall not commit adultery.' But I tell you that **anyone who looks at a woman lustfully has already committed adultery** with her in his heart.* (Matthew 5:27,28)

Negative thoughts about our spouse or marriage can severely undermine the relationship between a husband and wife. As an example, when Julaine and I reconciled after our separation, we agreed to take divorce out of our vocabulary and not even to say anything that would imply it. Many years later, after renovating an old house, we were going through a difficult time and I couldn't figure out what was going on. What I didn't know was that the challenges we were having were significant enough that Julaine was having thoughts about divorce. She didn't speak it, but she thought about it. She's always been committed to the marriage, so this was out of character for her. Once we both realized what was going on, she rejected the thoughts, we addressed the issue and got back on track. But, had she let the thoughts continue, we may very well have become yet another statistic. Thankfully, the Holy Spirit intervened!

Positive thoughts are powerful as well. Thoughts focused on God and his Word bring life and peace, and allow us to know God's will.

*The mind governed by the flesh is death, but **the mind governed by the Spirit is life and peace***. (Romans 8:6)

*Do not conform to the pattern of this world, but **be transformed by the renewing of your mind. Then you will be able to test and approve what God's will is**—his good, pleasing and perfect will.* (Romans 12:2)

Paul tells us what we are to think about:

*Finally, brothers and sisters, whatever is true, whatever is noble, whatever is right, whatever is pure, whatever is lovely, whatever is admirable—**if anything is excellent or praiseworthy—think about such things.*** (Philippians 4:8)

He also tells us what *not* to think about:

*Rather, clothe yourselves with the Lord Jesus Christ, and **do not think about how to gratify the desires of the flesh***. (Romans 13:14)

The more my thoughts have become aligned with God's Word, the more pleasant I've become to be around, and the better my relationship with Julaine has been. I can still let my thoughts drift, but I'm getting better at catching them before they take hold and cause damage to the relationship. It takes effort, intentionality, and diligence. I hope you find the same benefit as you apply these truths to your life.

Applying Faith in Your Marriage

Where are you causing or contributing to variance (disagreement) in your marriage? What steps will you take to reduce or eliminate variance?

Where are you causing or contributing to strife (overt conflict) in your marriage? What steps will you take to eliminate strife?

What words are you using that are interfering with your relationship? What steps will you take to change or eliminate them?

What negative thoughts have you been having about yourself, your spouse, and your marriage that are interfering with your relationship? What steps will you take to change or eliminate them?

Investing in Your Marriage

God commands us to take care of what we've been given; to be good stewards. (See Luke 19:11-26) How are you stewarding your marriage relationship? How much time, effort, or money do you invest in your marriage to keep it healthy? In my first marriage, and in the early part of my second marriage, I did not invest in our relationship. We did little to nothing to help us relate better to each other. We let other priorities in life to overtake focus on our marriage, and the marriage suffered as a result.

In addition to tending to and aligning with each other, which make ongoing deposits into the relationship, here are some other ways to consider investing in your marriage:

- ❖ Intentionally spending time alone with your spouse on a regular basis (eg, schedule time for daily conversations, weekly date nights, occasional yet regular getaways, etc.)
- ❖ Reading and studying a marriage or Christian book or participating together in a Bible study
- ❖ Attending marriage programs and retreats as often as possible, but at least once a year
- ❖ Engaging a marriage coach to identify relationship goals and move towards them, or scheduling routine sessions with a marriage counselor
- ❖ Connecting with an experienced married couple who can serve as a mentor couple to learn from their experience

Just like anything worthwhile in life, it takes time, effort, and at least some money. Your marriage is too important to skimp on, so do as many of these things as you are able on an ongoing basis, and you'll keep your marriage healthy and well. The key is to be intentional and consistent.

Applying Faith in Your Marriage

What are the ways you are you currently investing in your marriage relationship?

Of those, what would you like to do more of and how will you start to do them more?

What are different ways that you could invest in your marriage that you are not currently doing?

What is <u>one thing</u> that you are not currently doing to invest in your marriage, that you will commit to doing within the next 6 months? What steps will you take to make sure it happens?

CHAPTER 3: PRAYING TOGETHER IN MARRIAGE

Do you pray together as a couple...out loud?

If you answered no, you're not alone. It's been reported that less than 10% of Christian married couples pray together. I didn't early in my marriage, and even after we started to pray together, it took awhile to feel comfortable. But, I can tell you now that it is critical for couples to do it and it creates stronger intimacy.

Couples who pray together feel more connected. 68% of highly connected couples pray together regularly, compared to 73% of highly disconnected couples who don't pray regularly with their spouse (*The Good News About Marriage*, Shaunti Feldhahn)

Praying together is one of the most powerful things a married couple can do.

A Seed of Faith

---

*"Truly I tell you, if you have faith as small as a mustard seed, you can say to this mountain, 'Move from here to there,' and it will move.
Nothing will be impossible for you."*
-- Jesus (Matthew 17:20)

It takes faith to pray and according to Jesus in the verse above, with just a little faith, we can do amazing things. *"Faith is the substance of things hoped for, the evidence of things not seen."* (Hebrews 11:1) As followers of Jesus, we are to *"walk by faith, not by sight"* (2 Corinthians 5:7) and to *"watch, stand fast in the faith, be brave, be strong"* (1 Corinthians 16:13). *"Faith comes by hearing, and hearing by the word of God."* (Romans 10:17)

So, if our faith comes from hearing and standing on the Word of God (as written in the Bible), we should be able to overcome the challenges we face, even though we can't see a way past them. In the Scripture verse at the top of this page, Jesus tells us that if we have the faith of the smallest of seeds, we can move mountains, and that nothing will be impossible for us!

But, we are also warned that doubt works against faith and is responsible for the lack of results we may see from prayer.

*But when you ask, you must believe and not doubt, because **the one who doubts** is like a wave of the sea, blown and tossed by the wind. That person **should not expect to receive anything from the Lord**.*
(James 1:6,7)

Jesus told us that he is the key to overcoming trouble. By faith, we stand on his promises.

*"I have told you these things, so that in me you may have peace. **In this world you will have trouble. But take heart! I have overcome the world.**"* (John 16:33)

The Apostle John reinforces that it is our faith in Jesus that allows us to be victorious over challenges of this world.

*And this is the **victory** that has overcome the world—**our faith**.* (1 John 5:4)

By faith, we confidently approach God in prayer, believing that he will answer.

Applying Faith in Your Marriage

What resonates with you about faith as described in this section?

What challenges you or causes you to struggle about faith as described in this section? Pray, asking God to help you overcome your struggle to strengthen your faith.

What steps will you take to strengthen your faith so that your marriage is stronger? Who can help?

Models of Prayer from Jesus

> *"One day Jesus was praying in a certain place.*
> *When he finished, one of his disciples said to him,*
> *'Lord, teach us to pray, just as John taught*
> *his disciples.'"*
> -- Jesus (Luke 11:1)

Jesus modeled prayer for his disciples (and for us) several times. He frequently withdrew from his work and from others to get alone with God. It is good for us to do the same. We are also given a few other examples of how he prayed or how he suggested we pray.

Jesus provided direction on our posture when we pray.

"And when you pray, do not be like the hypocrites, for they love to pray standing in the synagogues and on the street corners to be seen by others. Truly I tell you, they have received their reward in full. **But when you pray, go into your room, close the door and pray to your Father, who is unseen.** *Then your Father, who sees what is done in secret, will reward you.* **And when you pray, do not keep on babbling** *like pagans, for they think they will be heard because of their many words. Do not be like them, for your Father knows what you need before you ask him.* (Matthew 6:5-8)

The key elements of prayer given here are: Pray in a private place. Pray to God the Father. Use few words. Believe that God knows what you need before asking him.

This does not negate praying with your spouse or other people. In the context of this passage, Jesus was telling his disciples not to pray long empty prayers in public to look good in front of other people. Praying with others is powerful and effective, which will be discussed in the next section.

When asked by his disciples about how to pray, Jesus responded:

"This, then, is how you should pray: 'Our Father in heaven, hallowed be your name, your kingdom come, your will be done, on earth as it is in heaven. Give us today our daily bread. And forgive us our debts, as we also have forgiven our debtors. And lead us not into temptation, but deliver us from the evil one.'" (Matthew 6:9-13)

The key elements of this prayer ("The Lord's Prayer") are: Praise the Father. Ask for his kingdom and will to be done on earth as in heaven. Ask for daily provision. Ask for forgiveness. Ask to keep from temptation and from evil.

After Jesus sent 72 of his disciples out to preach about God's kingdom and heal people (see Luke 10:1), He illustrates a prayer of praise.

At that time Jesus, full of joy through the Holy Spirit, said, "I praise you, Father, Lord of heaven and earth, because you have hidden these things from the wise and learned, and revealed them to little children. Yes, Father, for this is what you were pleased to do. (Luke 10:21)

The key elements of this prayer are: Praising God. Affirming what God has done.

When Jesus fed 5,000 men, plus all the women and children, with 5 loaves of bread and two fish, he illustrated another aspect of prayer.

Taking the five loaves and the two fish and looking up to heaven, he gave thanks and broke them. Then he gave them to the disciples to distribute to the people. (Luke 9:16)

The key elements of this prayer are: Lifting our eyes and what we have up to God (in this case, literally). Thanking God for them. (And/or asking God to bless them as reported in other versions.) Believing that God has answered (giving the baskets to the disciples to distribute to the people knowing God would provide enough for all).

When you read how Jesus prayed for himself, for his disciples, and for all believers in John 17, you'll notice that the key elements of his prayers are: Looking towards heaven. Praising God. Reminding God of what God said (promised) and what Jesus was sent to do (God's will). Asking what he desires for the disciples and other believers (protection, oneness/unity, to be with him in heaven).

Jesus praying in the Garden of Gethsemane, is another example of prayer.

Going a little farther, he fell with his face to the ground and prayed, "My Father, if it is possible, may this cup be taken from me. Yet not as I will, but as you will." (Matthew 26:39)

It reveals two elements of prayer: Sharing his desire with God. Yielding to God's will. This means accepting how God answers prayers, which may not be what we expect. We ask, but put the outcome in God's hands, trusting that he will answer in a way that is best for us.

Applying Faith in Your Marriage

What is most meaningful to you about what Jesus modeled in prayer?

What will you incorporate into your prayer life?

Six Layers of Prayer

"The prayer of a righteous person
is powerful and effective."
-- James (James 5:16)

Jesus makes us righteous (right with God) so that we can pray directly to God, although we still need to confess and repent of our sins as they occur so that sin doesn't get in the way of effective prayer.

What, exactly, is powerful and effective prayer? I've read and heard many answers, and there are numerous books about prayer. I will leave it up to you to go deeper on your own, if that's something you desire. In this section and the remainder of this chapter, I will briefly share my experience and perspective as an overview of some of the basics about prayer.

Growing up Catholic, most of my prayers were those given to me. The "Hail Mary," "Our Father" (also known as The Lords Prayer), and "Act of Contrition" were three that I memorized and prayed often. At that time and throughout much of my adult life, that's what prayer was to me – reciting memorized prayers that were given to me and praying them at specific times, usually during church or after going to confession as part of my repentance. We even had a memorized prayer that we said before meals, which I also taught my kids and still pray today.

It wasn't until after I committed my life to Jesus and began my journey of getting to know him at the age of 40, that I started to understand that prayer was much more than a set of memorized words. I have come to know that prayer is simply communion with

God. At its deepest level, it is a conversation with God that goes on continually, where I can ask anything and share my deepest emotions (which is not easy for me to do). As much as I'd like to have that kind of prayer all the time, I don't. It is a work in progress for me and probably always will be.

I am the type of guy who likes to have a plan, and formulas are appealing. That way, I know exactly what to do based on something known to work. There is no specific formula, but the Bible gives us some clues about prayer. As I pieced them together, I found that there are six layers of prayer.

Layer 1: Be in constant relationship with Jesus, and know and live by the Bible

Jesus said: *"If you abide in Me, and My words abide in you, you will ask what you desire, and it shall be done for you."* (John 15:7, New King James Version)

Layer 2: Ask Jesus or the Father what you desire in Jesus' name

Jesus said: "*You may ask me for anything in my name, and I will do it.*" (John 14:14)

"*You did not choose me, but I chose you and appointed you so that you might go and bear fruit—fruit that will last—and so that whatever you ask in my name the Father will give you.*" (John 15:16)

Layer 3: Align with what God would want for you, his will, what the Bible says is true and promised

The Apostle John wrote "*This is the confidence we have in approaching God: that if we ask anything according to his will, he hears us. And if we know that he hears us—whatever we ask—we know that we have what we asked of him.*" (1 John 5:14-15)

Layer 4: Pray as though the prayer is answered now; as though you already received it

Jesus said: *"Therefore I tell you, whatever you ask for in prayer, believe that you have received it, and it will be yours."* (Mark 11:24)

Layer 5: Believe and have faith that God will answer your prayer

Jesus said *"If you believe, you will receive whatever you ask for in prayer."* (Matthew 21:22)

Layer 6: Persevere in prayer and keep seeking and asking God

Then Jesus told his disciples a parable to show them that they should always pray and not give up. (Luke 18:1)

Layer 1 is foundational to all the other layers. It is critical that we are in an active relationship with Jesus and that God's Word is deeply embedded in us. Here's an example of a prayer reflecting the remaining five layers.

Father, in Jesus' name, I ask you to take away my worries. (Layer 2) *Your word says* (in Matthew 6:25-34) *that I don't need to worry because you know what I need and you will take care of me.* (Layer 3) *Thank you for taking away my worry.* (Level 4) *By faith, I believe that you are doing that even as I speak.* (Layer 5)

If I don't feel relief right away or within a short period of time, I will repeat the above as many times as needed until the worry goes away. (Layer 6)

When we pray incorporating these six layers, our prayers will be powerful and effective. In the next section, I will show how prayer is even more powerful when a married couple comes together.

Applying Faith in Your Marriage

How would you like to relate to God on a deeper level in prayer?

What value do you see in applying the six layers of prayer as you pray?

The Power of Two

Again, truly I tell you that if two of you on earth
agree about anything they ask for, it will be done
for them by my Father in heaven.
-- Jesus (Matthew 18:19)

You've likely heard the phrase, "there is power in numbers." In marriage, that number is two!

In the verse above and the two verses surrounding it, we get a clue into the power of a married couple coming together in prayer. When a couple gathers in Jesus' name, he promises to be with them. *"For where two or three gather in my name, there am I with them."* (Matthew 18:20) When Jesus is with you, there is power! Julaine and I usually start our prayer time together with something like: *Jesus, we gather in your name and thank you that because we do, you promise to be with us. Come sit with us.*

Next in verse 19 at the top of this page we are told that when "two" (a married couple) agree about anything they "ask for" (pray), God the Father will give it to them. That simply means that the couple needs to agree about what they are asking, keeping in mind the six layers of prayer mentioned the last section. But, by faith, believing that the Father will answer prayers, the couple can boldly present their shared desires to God.

Finally, in verse 18 we are told that a married couple has the power to bind (tie up, lock, attach) or loose (untie, let go of, release, break free from, unlock) anything, and it will be bound or loosed in heaven. *"Truly I tell you, whatever you bind on earth will be bound in heaven, and whatever you loose on earth will be loosed in heaven.*" I'm taking a little liberty here because this verse comes before Jesus mentions "two," so it applies to a follower of Jesus. But, I have to believe that Jesus intended it to be connected with two coming together in agreement in his name (verses 19 and 20). Since this verse talks about bringing heaven to earth, I think it applies mostly to the spiritual realm, including spiritual warfare, which will be addressed in the next chapter.

Think about the things you can bind. You can bind (attach) yourself to good things, such as the will and purposes of God, the Word of God, the truth of God, the mind of Jesus, the paths that God has set for you, God's love, or anything good from heaven. You can also bind (tie up) things that are harmful or not of God, such as pride, lust, accusation, judgement, and fear.

Similarly, you can loose (release) good things such as wisdom, understanding, knowledge, counsel, the spirit of God, the angelic realm or other good gifts from God. And, you can loose (break free from) harmful things, such as harsh or hard words spoken, wrong patterns of thinking, poor attitudes or beliefs, unhealthy habits, harmful desires or behaviors, or desire for revenge.

So, considering the six layers of prayer discussed in the last section, along with the three verses shared in this section, when a husband and wife abide in Jesus and embrace his words, gather in the name of Jesus, pray together (asking) in agreement about a need that is consistent with God's will (as written in the Bible) and believe, God will answer. Jesus promised that they can ask for anything and it will be given. That's real power!

Just imagine what can happen when you pray in agreement as a married couple. Would you like your marriage to be strengthened or restored? Be more connected? Take away anger, frustration, bitterness, resentment, or contempt? Have peace and joy? Overcome some adversity? Be aligned in parenting? Be in a better financial position? What if you first ask God what he wants you to pray about <u>before</u> you pray for anything?

Whatever you need, join together with your spouse, agree on what you want to ask, and pray! See what happens. If you don't see results, ask again, and again, and again, always together and always in agreement. And, be open to God answering your prayer in a way that you may not expect. Here are some examples of when Julaine and I agreed in prayer together, along with praying for the same thing individually.

Our church was raising money to purchase land for a building. Instead of just talking about what we should give, we decided to pray about it together and ask God how much he wanted us to give. At one point, we asked for God to give each of us an amount, which we agreed to write it down on paper before sharing it with each other. Both of us were given a number and when we shared it with each other, it was the same amount! It was also more than we'd ever given before and out of our comfort zone, but we committed to give that amount because we knew it was from God. Prayer answered.

On another occasion, we were downsizing. As we started our search, we were literally all over the map, not only geographically, but also in the type of house and property. After making an offer on a house that we thought was "the one," which was rejected, we decided to ask God what he wanted for us. We did this individually and together. (In hindsight, it would have saved us a lot of time had we done this first!)

After praying, we felt like we were to be in a community and Julaine sensed a location within a small geographic area. A few days later, a house came on the market in that specific area and we both felt it was where God wanted us to live. God had given me the terms for an offer before even viewing the house, so after seeing the house, as a way of confirming that we were to make an offer, I asked Julaine to pray about how much to offer. She came back with a number that was within $3,000 of the one I was given, so I asked her to pray again since it wasn't the same. After praying, she felt God was telling her to honor her husband, so we made an offer based on the terms God had given me. We live in that house today. Prayer answered.

Another time when our oldest son was battling brain cancer, we received a call from his wife that he was having repetitive seizures, which usually results in death or permanent disability. We flew from Columbus, Ohio to Phoenix, Arizona not knowing whether he would be alive when we got there, but praying that he would be. When we stepped into the hospital room, we were greeted by "Hi, Dad." That was the first time he had woken up since the seizures started. He had no significant deficits from the seizures. Prayer answered.

At one point, the tumor came back so he and his wife decided on surgery. The tumor was at the center of the brain, so the surgery was risky and the odds of our son coming out without permanent disability were low. We prayed in agreement before and during the surgery that God would guide the surgeon's hand and keep our son whole. The surgery was a success and our son was not adversely affected by the surgery. Prayers answered. Now, I don't deny that the surgeon was gifted, because he was known for having success and taking on cases where others wouldn't, but I also believe God put that surgeon in our son's path at just the right time.

A last example I will share is that we've been praying in agreement with each other for our grown children to commit their life to Jesus. All of them fell away from the church after leaving home and had not gone back. We prayed for our oldest son as he was "seeking the real truth" and we witnessed him invite Jesus into his heart during a time when he was being prayed over for healing. He died a couple of months later. At his gravesite, in my spirit and with a gust of wind, I heard God say "He is with me." After at least 10 years of praying, one of our other sons called me and asked me if I would baptize him so that he could then baptize his wife and oldest daughter. Prayers answered. We are still praying for our other children and their spouses, expectantly waiting for the day when they turn their hearts toward Jesus and walk with him.

Prayers in agreement aren't always on this order of magnitude, but when we pray in agreement together, we have faith that it is powerful and that God will respond.

Are prayers always answered?

One of the biggest challenges with praying is questioning whether God will answer. That's actually where our faith comes in – believing that he will answer. I've learned that there are so many dynamics with prayer that sometimes we don't know how God answers, but, by faith, I believe that he answers all prayers one way or another. I heard a pastor say that God always answers prayers in one of three ways – yes, no, and not now (no response yet). We all want a "yes" to our prayers, but if we take the position that God always has our best interest in mind, we can accept his answer. If he said "yes" to all we ask, chances are it wouldn't all be good for us.

I have no doubt God hears my prayers because, after all, he knows everything. He knows what I'm going to pray before I do, but waits for me to express it. God wants me to be communing with him! I've learned that the answer might not be what I want or it may not come for a long time. Here are some examples.

In 2012, our oldest son died at the age of 30 as a result of brain cancer, ending a 5-year battle. We prayed for him to live, but he didn't. However, there were moments during his battle when our prayers were answered, as shared earlier. Additionally, before chemo and radiation started, a pastor prayed over him for healing in the name of Jesus. Six months later he was cancer-free and remained that way for a year and a half. What is noteworthy is that the doctors only expected the treatment to slow down the growth of the tumor, or possibly result in a small amount of regression. But, after six months the cancer was completely gone! I attribute that to answered prayers through the healing power of Jesus.

One of our other sons became estranged with us at the age of 19. I won't go into the details, but we prayed for reconciliation almost immediately after he left and said he would never come back. We kept praying individually and together, not daily, but frequently. It was a void in our life that we desperately wanted God to fill. Julaine reached out to our son periodically, but without response. It didn't seem like God was answering our prayers. However, after 10 years of virtually no contact, he reconnected with us, and our relationship continues to grow as we catch up on lost years. Another prayer answered.

During each of these times, we asked God what we wanted. We kept asking. We put the outcome in God's hands and were willing to accept whatever that might be. We were thankful when the prayer was answered, even if it wasn't when or how we wanted it to be.

We have many other examples of prayers where the answer was "no," or where prayers didn't seem to be answered, but eventually were. We have others that are still in the "not yet" phase where we haven't seen the answer. But, we keep asking!

Applying Faith in Your Marriage

What resonated with you in this section?

What challenged you?

If you are not already doing so, what can you do to start praying with your spouse?

What steps can you take to start praying *in agreement* to unleash the "power of two" in your life and marriage?

What's keeping you from boldly asking God for what you want for your life and marriage?

Rejoice, Praise, Give Thanks

---

*Rejoice always, pray continually, give thanks
in all circumstances; for this is God's will
for you in Christ Jesus.*
-- The Apostle Paul (1 Thessalonians 5:16-18)

It is easy in marriage (and life) to find fault, look at the negative, and criticize, or at least it has been for me. Eventually, the negative overshadows the positive, so it is important to focus on the positive, no matter how small. Rejoicing, praising God, and giving thanks helps you keep focused on the good, on God, and not on the negative. When you do these three things regularly, God promises that you will experience peace.

Do not be anxious about anything, but in every situation, by prayer and petition, with thanksgiving, present your requests to God. And the peace of God, which transcends all understanding, will guard your hearts and your minds in Christ Jesus. (Philippians 4:6

Applying what was discussed in the last section, imagine how effective it would be for a married couple to rejoice, praise, and give thanks *in agreement with each other* as a form of prayer even when facing challenges! It breaks something in the atmosphere.

As a practical matter to help you do this, and to remind you about the positives, it may be helpful to keep a marriage praise and gratitude journal with a running list of things that you are thankful for, especially those things relating to each other as spouses and things happening in your marriage. Not only will this will give you something to guide your time for praise and prayer, but you can also refer to it when you are going through a rough patch to remind yourself of the good that has happened.

Finally, most of the book of Psalms contains prayers, and you'll see a variety of them as you read it. Some are prayers of praise, some are prayers of thanksgiving, some are pleas or petitions, and much more. The entire book illustrates the breadth of how you can pray. I've even used them, as well as other scripture verses when I pray. I'll share specific examples in the next section.

Applying Faith in Your Marriage

What are some of the things right now that you can rejoice about, praise God for, or give thanks for? After writing them down, lift them up in prayer, rejoicing, praising, and thanking God!

In what ways can you make rejoicing, praising, and giving thanks a part of your normal prayer individually, and as a married couple?

Praying Scripture for Specific Needs

---

*This is the confidence we have in approaching God:
that if we ask anything according to his will, he
hears us. And if we know that he hears us—
whatever we ask—we know that we have
what we asked of him.*
-- The Apostle John (1 John 5:14,15)

As previously discussed, when two come together in prayer and belief, it unlocks power and God hears and responds, especially when a couple prays Scripture for specific needs because they are praying according to his will. This approach can be used to ask the Father or to battle against things that are not aligned with God's nature and desire for us. We can preface the prayer by saying "It is written" or "God, your Word says," or something similar, to declare that it is a truth from God, consistent with his will.

Below are examples of praying Scripture that I developed to address common issues individuals and married couples face. If these don't resonate with you for the topic listed, search Scripture for verses that speak to your heart while addressing what you are praying for or the issue you are facing. You can even read the scripture verse itself as a form of prayer and ask for it in your life or marriage. I often find it helpful to pray out loud, especially if I am praying with my wife. It also helps me to stay focused and slows me down to concentrate on what I am praying, compared to when I pray silently.

Anxiety

God, your Word says that we are not to be anxious about anything, that it only causes grief, pain and unrest. We are tired of feeling overwhelmed, being anxious, and taking it all on ourselves. So, as your Word instructs us, we are now casting all our anxiety on you. We are weary and give our burdens to you, Jesus, because you promised to carry them. (See Psalm 139:23, Ecclesiastes 2:22-23, Philippians 4:6, 1 Peter 5:7, Matthew 11:28)

Anger

Father, forgive us for getting angry and giving the devil a foothold. We repent of being angry and want to get rid of the anger. As your Word says, help us to be quick to listen and slow to speak. We want to have the righteousness that you desire. In the name of Jesus, we bind the power and effects of the harsh words we have spoken so that they no longer have control over us and others. We replace our anger with compassion, kindness, humility, gentleness, and patience. (See Ephesians 4:26-27, Colossians 3:8,12, James 1:19-21)

Arguing

God, your Word instructs us to avoid arguing, strife, discord, and dissention. Father, remove all division between us and bring us together once again as one. Fill us with your humility, gentleness, and patience so that we live with one another in love and are at peace with each other. (See Proverbs 20:3, Philippians 2:14-15, Galatians 5:19-21,26, Ephesians 4:2, Romans 12:18)

Confusion

God, your Spirit lives in us as our guide and counselor, giving us perfect knowledge, so there is no place for confusion.

Your Word says that, as believers, we have the mind of Christ and that our mind is governed by the Spirit, giving us life and peace. Right now, we aren't feeling life and peace, so we stand against and bind all confusion, and invite your Spirit to take its place so that we can gain clarity. (See 1 Corinthians 14:33, 2:15-16, Romans 8:5-6)

Discontent

Father, help us to be content in all of our circumstances like Paul was able to do. Show us the source of our discontent and the way out of it so that we can walk in the freedom you desire for us. (See Philippians 4:11)

Doubt

Father, forgive us for doubting You. We do not want to be like a wave blown and tossed by the wind. Show us how to remove doubt so that we can stand strong in faith and believe fully that you will come through for us. (See James 1:6)

Fear

We will not be afraid. God, we stand on the truth that your Word says that your perfect love casts out fear and that you have not given us a spirit of fear, but that you have given us a spirit of power, love and a sound mind. Fear has no place in us, so in the name of Jesus, we bind and banish it from us. (See 1 John 4:18, 2 Timothy 1:7)

Financial Challenges

Father, forgive us for focusing on money instead of you. As your Word says, help us to be content with what we have, knowing that you will never leave us. Shine your light on the path that will lead us out of this financial challenge we are facing so that we have no debt outstanding, except our love for others. (See Hebrews 13:5, Romans 13:8, 2 Corinthians 8:9. Also, see prayers for worry, anxiety, and fear.)

Hope

God, you are the God of hope. Your Word and your promises are the anchor of our souls, and you are faithful. We stand on the truth that your Word says that we can place our hope in you and that all things work together for good. As you promise, let us overflow with hope by the power of the Holy Spirit. (See Romans 8:28, 15:12-13, Hebrews 6:18-19)

Joy

Father, your Word says that you can fill me with joy as I trust in you. I ask you to fill me with joy overflowing by the power of the Holy Spirit. (Romans 15:13)

Parenting

Father, help us to agree on how to parent our children. Guide us in what we teach them about the world and about you. Help us to avoid causing them to be bitter or resentful, so they don't become discouraged, but show us the proper amount and types of discipline so that we have peace and they bring delight to us and to you. Give us the strength to be firm when we need to be, but also to know when we need to extend grace and treat them with gentleness. Help us to raise our children as you would have us do, and help us to be the parents you intend us to be. (See Ephesians 6:4, Proverbs 13:25, 22:6, 29:17, Colossians 3:21)

Peace

Father, we are feeling overwhelmed right now and we know that's not where you want us. We need you. We stand on your promise of peace, which transcends all understanding and guards our hearts and minds. Your Word says that we will have trouble, but that Jesus overcame the world. He is our peace. In faith, we stand on the truth that Jesus is victorious and, as a result, we are victorious. Help us to walk in that victory and experience the peace that comes from it. (See Philippians 4:7, John 6:33, Ephesians 2:14-15)

Sadness (Depression)

Father, we are feeling sad and depressed right now. But, we stand on the truth that your Word says that the Holy Spirit will give us joy in the midst of suffering. We ask you to fill us with joy as a fruit of the Spirit living in us. Anoint us with the oil of joy. (See 1 Thessalonians 1:6, Galatians 5:22-23, Hebrews 1:9)

Strength

Father, we are feeling weak right now and don't have the strength to continue. It feels impossible. But, we stand on the truth of your Word that says that your power is made perfect in our weakness and that it is Christ who strengthens us. So, we ask you to give us strength right now in our weakness so that your power will rest on us. (See 2 Corinthians 12:8-9, Philippians 4:13)

Suffering

Father, we know that your Word says that suffering builds character and ultimately produces hope. If we are suffering for those purposes, give us strength to endure the suffering and to do it with joy. Help us, like Paul, to see our suffering as not worth comparing to your glory that will be revealed in us. If we are suffering needlessly, we ask you to remove our suffering like you have for so many people, or show us the root of our suffering and how we can handle it. (See Romans 5:1-5, 8:18)

Unbelief

Jesus, we believe you are all that God's Word says you are, and that you are the same today as you were when you walked the earth as a human. As you did for the father of the boy who was having seizures, help us overcome our unbelief so that it does not hinder our prayers or weaken our faith. Your Word says that it only takes the faith of a mustard seed to move a mountain. Surely, we have at least that much faith, so we ask you to move the mountain in front of us. (See Matthew 17:20, Mark 9:21-24)

Unity

Father, we feel divided right now and we aren't on the same page. Your Word says that you have joined us together as husband and wife and that nothing will separate us. Thank you that we are one with each other and one with you. We ask you to remove all division and show us how to align with each other and be in unity as you have designed us to be in marriage. (See Matthew 19:4-6)

Wisdom (Discernment)

Father, your Word says that you will give wisdom generously to those who ask. We are coming before you now and ask that you give us wisdom generously regarding this situation (specify what it is), so that we know how to proceed. (See James 1:5)

Worry

God, your Word says that we are not to worry about anything because we are valuable to you and you know what we need. We choose not to worry and in the name of Jesus we bind and banish worry from us. Worry has no place in us as children of God. (See Matthew 6:25-27, 31-34)

Applying Faith in Your Marriage

Which of the specific prayers relate to something you are going through? When will you start praying them or the scripture verses to address your need?

What scripture verses can you use to create a prayer for a specific need you have right now that wasn't listed?

Chapter 4: Battling Together in Marriage

Given the number of struggling marriages and high divorce rate, I don't think anyone would argue that marriage is under attack. There are many things that may pull a couple apart, whether it be a person (or people), busyness, other priorities, addiction, or any number of other sources of division or conflict that gets in the way of a healthy marriage.

To counter these pressures, in addition to living biblically and praying together, there is one more thing I believe is critical for a married couple to do to stay together – battle effectively for their marriage and for each other.

The Setting for Marriage

"For our struggle is not against flesh and blood, but against the rulers, against the authorities, against the powers of this dark world and against the spiritual forces of evil in the heavenly realms."
-- The Apostle Paul (Ephesians 6:12)

We Have An Enemy And We Are In A Battle

Before discussing how a husband and wife can battle together, we need to understand the setting (battleground) for marriage. Through Paul, in the verse above, God tells us that we have an enemy and that we are at war with the unseen realm that shows up in our physical realm. We are in the midst of battle on a daily basis. I think everyone would agree that all of us have struggles, some bigger than others and some that occur more frequently than others. As the verse above states, these struggles, or battles, are not against each other ("flesh and blood"). They are often against the kingdom of darkness.

This may be a new concept to you or it may not be a part of your belief system. It hasn't always been something I believed or that I have taken into account either, but I have come to embrace it based on personal experiences. Before you close the book and throw out everything you've read so far, I urge you to stick with me, keeping your mind open to the possibility that this may be true. At least read through the chapter before you dismiss it. I am not saying that every difficulty in life and marriage has a spiritual war underpinning, but if it's not considered, people may suffer needlessly.

The premise of the marriage book, *Love and War*, by John and Stasi Eldredge, is that we live in a love story set in the midst of a war. It is a battle for our heart, mind, body, soul, and spirit...and our marriage. God gives us the option of choosing him, or choosing ourselves or worldly ways over him. In the verse at the top of the page, we are told that we do not battle against flesh and blood, but against an unseen spiritual world. This may seem strange to you (it did to me when I first heard it), but if you start to pay attention to what's going on in the world around you and how many atrocities are unexplainable, you'll begin to see it.

The first time I became aware of the spiritual battle was when my oldest son was at the late stages of his battle with brain cancer. He was bedridden by then and one day it looked like he was being tormented. He was uncomfortable and I could see terror in his eyes. He was also trying to swat things away that weren't there and would push back in his bed like he was trying to avoid something.

Coincidentally, I had just finished reading a book on spiritual warfare. I'm not even sure why I was reading it at that time. But, I felt that he might be under spiritual attack. So, I asked him if I could try to cast away whatever might be there. He agreed and we gathered the family members present around his bed. I asked them to simply pay attention to any spirits that they felt might be there and tell me. Most of the family members were not followers of Jesus, so I said that I would take authority over the spirits in Jesus' name as we identified them.

I simply said "In the name of Jesus, I bind the spirit of oppression and I send it off property. In the name of Jesus, I bind the spirit of torment, and I send it off property." I did that for each spirit that we felt was attacking him until we didn't sense any more. After I did this, my son was at complete peace, no longer exhibiting the agitated behavior he did before. I don't understand how it worked, but it did. It affirmed for me that there is a spiritual war and that we can have victory over it by the authority of Jesus.

We gain a better understanding of the battle setting specific to marriage through several passages from the Bible.

Married Couples As Image-Bearers Are Targeted

A man and woman are made in God's image. Together (male and female), a husband and wife represent the fullness of God.

> *So God created mankind in his own image, in the image of God he created them; male and female he created them.* (Genesis 1:27)

Satan Is Out to Destroy God's People and Marriage

Satan is even more outraged by a Christian married couple since they are the "offspring" of Eve *and* are those who testify about Jesus (See Revelation 12:17). He will do everything possible to create division and break up a marriage.

> God said: *And **I will put enmity between you** [Satan] **and the woman, and between your offspring and hers**; he will crush your head, and you will strike his heel."* (Genesis 3:15)

> *Be alert and of sober mind. Your enemy **the devil prowls around like a roaring lion looking for someone to devour.*** (1 Peter 5:8)

Don't miss this point. God tells us through Peter that the devil is always on the prowl and always looking to devour his prey, those who love God and follow Jesus. No wonder that we have difficulties in this world and that marriages are failing. Many couples are unaware that this is happening. I was for a long time too!

Our Battle Is Not Against Our Spouse

When I first heard someone tell me that my wife is not my enemy (based on Ephesians 6:12), it shifted a lot of things for me. Although I knew she wasn't my enemy, I didn't realize how often I responded to her as though she *was* my enemy. When I consider that we are on the same team and that what I see from her may be responses out of deeper wounds or from the enemy controlling her thoughts, feelings, words (and tone) or reactions, it shifts my perspective and how I respond.

Jesus illustrated this for us when he told His disciples that he was going to suffer and be killed.

> Peter took him aside and began to rebuke him. "Never, Lord!" he said. "This shall never happen to you!" Jesus turned and said to Peter, "Get behind me, Satan! You are a stumbling block to me; you do not have in mind the concerns of God, but merely human concerns." (Matthew 16:22,23)

Clearly, Peter was not Satan, so Jesus was speaking to what was causing Peter to say what he was saying. He was speaking to what was happening in the unseen spiritual realm. We are to do the same. I am not suggesting that when we have a confrontation with our spouse, we should say what Jesus said. In fact, that would cause a lot of conflict. While we don't have the same ability to discern the spiritual realm that Jesus had, the Holy Spirit in us can reveal what spirit is at work. Then we can speak against that spirit, just as Jesus did in the case with Peter, although we would do it in the name of Jesus, on His authority.

Additionally, John shared three things that we should look for that are contrary to God:

> For everything in the world—**the lust of the flesh, the lust of the eyes, and the pride of life—comes not from the Father** but from the world. (1 John 2:16)

So, based on this verse, if you see or hear your spouse desiring for things of this world that may interfere with your marriage, or looking outside of your marriage for fulfillment, or doing something out of pride, try to remember that the lusts and pride are not from God. Then, you can pray to break the hold that those things have on your spouse, and even talk with your spouse about what you are sensing about the potential underlying source of your spouse's desires. It is important to do this gently and take care not to use this verse as a way of controlling your spouse instead of helping to open his or her eyes to what might be happening.

Our Mind Is The Battleground

Consider the challenges you have with your spouse, or anyone else for that matter. From where do the issues originate? If you evaluate them thoroughly, I am almost certain that you will trace the root to a thought. That may be part of why Paul instructs us to renew our mind.

> **Do not conform to the pattern of this world, but be transformed by the renewing of your mind.** Then you will be able to test and approve what God's will is—his good, pleasing and perfect will. (Romans 12:2)

He also provides some instruction about what things we should be thinking about, promising that when we do, we will experience peace.

> *Finally, brethren, whatever things are true, whatever things are noble, whatever things are just, whatever things are pure, whatever things are lovely, whatever things are of good report, if there is any virtue and if there is anything praiseworthy—meditate [think] on these things.* *The things which you learned and received and heard and saw in me, these do,* *and the God of peace will be with you.* (Philippians 4:8,9)

When we consider that our brain controls our physical and emotional state, what we put in our mind has significant influence on our entire being, as well as our marriage.

So, what does all of this mean? It means that there is a war going on that we can't see. As a Christian married couple, you are targets of an attack from an unseen enemy that is relentless and hates you. He would like nothing better than to destroy your marriage and family. He is your real enemy, not your spouse. He wants to control your thoughts, so that he can control every other aspect of your life. You can stand against him by controlling your thoughts and renewing your mind through God's Word. We will get into more specifics in the following pages.

Applying Faith in Your Marriage

As you look back on the challenges you've had in your marriage through the lens of being in a spiritual war, what do you see?

Knowing this now, how might you have responded differently to what happened?

Which of the concepts presented in this section are new to you, and how might that impact your view of challenges in your marriage?

Which of the concepts are hard for you to accept? Pray, and ask God for wisdom to help you understand them.

Preparing for Battle

For though we live in the world, we do not wage
war as the world does. The weapons we fight with
are not the weapons of the world.
-- The Apostle Paul (2 Corinthians 10:3)

Knowing that marriage is under attack and we are at war, it is important for us to prepare for battle. But how? The verse above tells us that the weapons we fight with are not the weapons of the world. So, what are they?

Our real battle is not against each other even though it appears that way. It is in the spiritual realm, so the weapons we would normally use won't work. These include logic, intellect, reasoning, and arguing, as well as any physical efforts to fend off attacks. I am <u>not</u> saying that these won't ever work to resolve differences, but if there is underlying spiritual warfare, they won't be effective.

Two scripture passages let us know how to prepare for battle, revealing eight keys to being prepared:

*On the contrary, they have divine power to demolish strongholds. We demolish arguments and every pretension that sets itself up against the knowledge of God, and we **take captive every thought to make it obedient to Christ**. (2 Corinthians 10:4,5)*

*Therefore **put on the full armor of God**, so that when the day of evil comes, you may be able to stand your ground, and after you have done everything, to stand. Stand firm then, with the **belt of truth** buckled around your waist, with the **breastplate*** *of righteousness* in place, and with **your feet fitted with the readiness that comes from the gospel of peace**. *In addition to all this, take up the* **shield of faith**, *with which you can extinguish all the flaming arrows of the evil one. Take the* **helmet of salvation** *and the* **sword of the Spirit, which is the word of God**. *And* **pray in the Spirit** *on all occasions with all kinds of prayers and requests. With this in mind, be alert and always keep on praying for all the Lord's people.* (Ephesians 6:13-18)

1. Turn Our Thoughts Over To Jesus

Since the main battleground is our mind, controlling our thoughts is critical. Our thoughts influence our attitudes, which influence our beliefs, which influence our behaviors, which impact how we interact with our spouse and everyone around us. So, we are instructed to take thoughts captive, which means to become aware of our thoughts, catching them. Once we do, we can turn them over to Jesus, making them obedient to him. It is about what we choose to do with our thoughts – we can let them take hold and do damage, or we can give them over to Jesus so that they don't result in harm.

For example, let's say that I see an attractive woman and I catch myself extending my glance, maybe even fantasizing about her. In that moment, I have a choice. I can either let my thoughts continue, which would likely lead to lustful thoughts, eye contact, initiating conversation, and possibly eventually turning into an affair if I don't stop the train of thoughts. The enemy to my marriage (and to God) would like nothing more than for me to go down that path. In fact, he is likely the one walking me down it in my mind, even though I would hear it as my own thoughts.

But there is another path I could take, one that would help me counter the enemy's attack. I can give my thoughts to Jesus. So, after catching myself extending my glance, I can choose to stop in that moment. I would tell myself something like: *No, God gave me Julaine as my perfect provision and I have eyes only for her. I love her and I love God, so I am not going to continue to think about this woman. Jesus, by faith, I give these thoughts to you and I ask you to take them away and replace them with what you would have me think about instead.* The key is not to let the thought take hold.

2. Truth

We are to put on the belt of truth. In ancient times, most of the armor was secured by the belt, which also kept the warrior's private parts from being exposed. Jesus is the truth. (John 14:6) So, to me, this means that we need to know and embrace Jesus and all that is written about him in the Bible as true. We stand on the truth and believe it grounds us in spiritual battles to keep us from being exposed.

3. Righteousness

Once we've invited Jesus into our hearts, he makes us righteous with God. He was sent to reconcile us to God. Because of Jesus, we are righteous, even when we sin or even rebel against God, although it's good for us to turn from our ways and ask forgiveness so that sin doesn't cause a break in the armor. I like to think of the breastplate of righteousness protecting my heart. There are many lies, accusations, and judgements that might be made about me, or even that I think about myself, which may cause me to have doubts about my relationship with God. But, I can stand on the truth that Jesus made me righteous and it restores my confidence and uplifts my spirit.

4. Gospel of Peace

In ancient times, the shoes were an important piece of armor. They provided stability and helped the warrior to stand firm in hand-to-hand combat. We can do the same as we find our peace that surpasses understanding through Jesus (Philippians 4:7). So, when we are faced with adversity, we can stand firm, resting in the peace that Jesus provides, knowing that he is bigger than anything we are facing.

5. Faith

The shield is the only piece of protective armor that a person has control over in battle. The warrior can move the shield towards the direction of the enemy threat to keep the arrows from hitting him. Similarly, our faith is to be our shield, protecting us from assaults of our unseen enemy. When we hear ourselves or others saying something (lies, accusations, judgements, etc.) against us that is not consistent with who God says we are (our identity in Christ), we can deflect and reject it. *No, that's not true. I reject it. I am a child of God. I am fearfully and wonderfully made.* We do this, by faith, even when we think there may be a little bit of truth in what they are saying.

6. Salvation

The helmet obviously protects the head. Similarly, the helmet of salvation covers the head and protects the brain, or mind. Jesus saved us. We can't earn it and don't deserve it. Once we invite Jesus into our heart, he saves us from eternal separation from God that we would have otherwise experienced because of our sins. So, we don't let anyone, even ourselves, tell us lies about whether we are saved. We are saved. End of story.

7. Word of God

The only offensive weapon we have is the Word of God. We are told: *For the word of God is alive and active. Sharper than any double-edged sword, it penetrates even to dividing soul and spirit, joints and marrow; it judges the thoughts and attitudes of the heart.* (Hebrews 4:12) What this means to me is that speaking the Word of God (as written in the Bible) will have power and will overcome any circumstances facing me. I overcome lies or whatever I'm feeling attacked with, by speaking the truth from the Bible.

8. Prayer

While prayer is not part of the "armor of God," it is closely linked. Paul tells us to use all kinds of prayers and to pray continually (1 Thessalonians 5:17). Suffice it to say that praying is needed to win spiritual battles in addition to the armor and weapons listed above.

Prayer is different than battle. Prayer is asking God to lead you, guide you, protect you, deliver you, reveal what's really at work, give you strength, provide peace, or something else that will help you to deal with circumstances in the moment or over time. If we pray for something God has already given us authority and power to overcome, it may seem like our prayers aren't being answered. God won't overstep the authority that's in place, so we need to exercise the authority Jesus gave us.

Battle is fighting the spiritual opposition, the things that you can't see. It is speaking against what God reveals to you or what you sense is underneath what you are seeing in front of you. It is taking authority in the name of Jesus and using scripture verses as your sword. For the sake of your life and marriage, it is important that you do both, pray and battle. Not that we need to look for a demon around every corner, but just as Jesus did when he walked the earth as a man, we need to handle the spiritual realm as it is revealed. The remainder of this chapter is intended to show you how.

As I'm sure you can see, the better we know the Bible, the more effectively prepared we will be for the spiritual battle that we encounter every day. Knowing the Bible equips us for employing the full armor of God.

I don't claim to know how this works, but, by faith, I believe this to be true. I put on the full armor of God each morning by praying Ephesians 6:13-18 (or some version of it) as I sit on the edge of the bed before I get up. Plus, I declare it at different points throughout the day when I expect to confront a potentially difficult situation. When I forget to do it, I notice that things seem a bit off. I don't understand how, but I believe that it helps protect me, so I do it in faith.

Here's an example of what I pray after I wake up, but before I get out of bed:

Father, thank you for waking me up to experience another day. I give you my spirit, soul, and body, my heart, mind, and will, to be one with you as Jesus is one with you. I cover myself with the blood of Jesus to release any and all claims the enemy has had on me. I once again put on the full armor of God. I put on the belt of truth, breastplate of righteousness, shoes with the gospel of peace, helmet of salvation, and I take up the shield of faith and the sword of the Spirit, which is the Word of God. I pray at all times in the spirit with all prayer and supplication. Father, lead me through this day. Amen.

Applying Faith in Your Marriage

Which of the eight components described in this section are most challenging for you to embrace? Pray, asking God to help you overcome your unbelief and to help you "see" the importance of them.

What steps can you take to deploy these eight components in your daily life and marriage?

Battle Strategies in Marriage

"May God himself, the God of peace, sanctify you through and through. May your whole spirit, soul and body be kept blameless at the coming of our Lord Jesus Christ."
-- The Apostle Paul (1 Thessalonians 5:23)

As humans, our being consists of body, soul (mind), and spirit. Much of our attention focuses on how to address issues of the body and mind, but not the spirit. For marriage health, all three need to be addressed. However, if the spiritual causes are addressed, physical or mental issues may decrease or resolve, indicating that there may be an unknown underlying spiritual root to them. Even though it may not seem like it, our main battle is spiritual, so it is important to have effective strategies in place to fight successfully for our marriage.

Here are six battle strategies in marriage a husband and wife can deploy that will reduce the severity and frequency of challenges, allowing them to stand their ground against attempts by the enemy to create division in their relationship.

Strategy 1: Seek God, Be Alert, Submit, and Resist

Jesus said that the greatest commandment is to love God with all of our heart, soul, and mind. To effectively battle, God needs to be first. We are told that if we seek him first, we don't need to worry. We are also told to be alert for the devil, but to submit ourselves to God and resist the devil, which will cause him to flee from us.

[Jesus said] *So do not worry, saying, 'What shall we eat?' or 'What shall we drink?' or 'What shall we wear?' For the pagans run after all these things, and your heavenly Father knows that you need them. But* **seek first his kingdom and his righteousness, and all these things will be given to you as well.** *Therefore do not worry about tomorrow, for tomorrow will worry about itself. Each day has enough trouble of its own.* (Matthew 6:31-34)

Be alert and of sober mind. *Your enemy the devil prowls around like a roaring lion looking for someone to devour.* (1 Peter 5:8)

Submit *yourselves, then, to God.* **Resist** *the devil, and he will flee from you.* (James 4:7, NIV)

Strategy 2: Believe and Have Faith

Faith is our main protection ("shield") against the schemes of the enemy forces. (See Ephesians 6:16) Whenever we are confronted with anything that steals, kills, or destroys our peace, joy, love, or anything else of God, and we stand against it in faith, God's Word tells us we will be victorious.

This is the victory that has overcome the world, even our faith. Who is it that overcomes the world? Only the one who believes that Jesus is the Son of God. (1 John 5:4,5)

Strategy 3: Stand on Your Authority in Jesus

We are given everything we need in life and marriage through Jesus. His shed blood washes us clean from our sins. He has given us authority to overcome the enemy. His name is above all names and every force against you and your marriage must bow to the name of Jesus.

*[Jesus said] **I have given you authority** to trample on snakes and scorpions and **to overcome all the power of the enemy**; nothing will harm you. (Luke 10:19)*

*Therefore God exalted him to the highest place and gave him the name that is above every name, that **at the name of Jesus every knee should bow, in heaven and on earth and under the earth**, and every tongue acknowledge that Jesus Christ is Lord, to the glory of God the Father. (Philippians 2:9-11)*

*And these signs will accompany those who believe: **In my [Jesus] name they will drive out demons; they will speak in new tongues; they will pick up snakes with their hands; and when they drink deadly poison, it will not hurt them at all; they will place their hands on sick people, and they will get well.**" (Mark 16:17,18)*

What this means is that when we as followers of Jesus invoke his name and authority, any enemy forces opposing us must bow to him. They must relent and give up control. It's up to us to exercise the authority given to us.

Strategy 4: Stay in the Spirit

Satan is very cunning (see Genesis 3:1). He and those in his army are often very subtle in how they operate. They cause us to believe that things which go against God are normal. But, God tells us that we have a choice to either follow the Spirit of God (living in ways pleasing to him), or we can follow our own desires and the ways of the world. We can't do both, if we want to stay in the Spirit and effectively battle the enemy through his power.

We are instructed not to hinder the move of the Holy Spirit.

*So I say, **walk by the Spirit, and you will not gratify the desires of the flesh**. For the flesh desires what is contrary to the Spirit, and the Spirit what is contrary to the flesh.* (Galatians 5:16-17)

We are provided a list of some behaviors that get in the way of the Holy Spirit in us because he can't coexist when they are present in our lives.

*The acts of the flesh are obvious: **sexual immorality, impurity and debauchery; idolatry and witchcraft; hatred, discord, jealousy, fits of rage, selfish ambition, dissensions, factions and envy; drunkenness, orgies, and the like.*** (Galatians 5:19-21)

When we are avoiding these, the Holy Spirit can flow freely, and we express his "fruit."

*But the fruit of the Spirit **is love, joy, peace, forbearance, kindness, goodness, faithfulness, gentleness and self-control**.* (Galatians 5:22)

If you are struggling with something in your marriage, evaluate whether one or more of the "acts of the flesh" are present. If so, the Holy Spirit can't work in you. Immediately stop doing those things, repent of having done them, ask God to forgive you, and then turn your focus back on him by lining up your attitude and behaviors with what is pleasing to God. (See Appendix 1 "Enemy Arrows and Kingdom Weapons" for an expanded list of things that stand in the way of the Holy Spirit and those that are aligned with him.)

Immersing yourself in God's Word is helpful in getting back in the Spirit. Expressing love also allows the Spirit to flow freely in us and through us to others.

Strategy 5: Love Each Other

Love is the central theme throughout the Bible. We are told that God is love (1 John 4:8), and we are instructed to love each other. Nowhere is this more critical than in marriage. It seems like a no brainer, but at times, it is easier said than done. However, loving our spouse without expecting anything in return can overcome many challenges we face. Paul provides some guidance around love.

> *Love must be sincere. Hate what is evil; cling to what is good. Be devoted to one another in love. Honor one another above yourselves. Never be lacking in zeal, but keep your spiritual fervor, serving the Lord. Be joyful in hope, patient in affliction, faithful in prayer.* (Romans 12:9-12)

As we seek God first, his love fills us so that we can love our spouse. Love covers a multitude of sins (1 Peter 4:8), so love can overtake the "sin" the enemy is trying to use against a husband and wife. Jesus said that there is no greater love than to lay down your life for a friend (John 15:13), so when we set aside our agenda for our spouse, we are showing love, which will allow us to overcome the issue between us. We are told to overcome evil with good (love) (Romans 12:21). Keep in mind that we are not saying our spouse is evil, but we are recognizing evil is at work, so we overcome it through love.

Strategy 6: Forgive Each Other

One of the single most important things a married couple can do is to seek and give forgiveness quickly and often. Unforgiveness can quickly lead to bitterness and ultimately to contempt, which is a killer to the marriage relationship. Unforgiveness opens the door for division in marriage because when it is present, a couple is at variance, which makes it difficult for the Holy Spirit to flow in their marriage. (See Galatians 5:16-26)

> *Bear with each other and **forgive one another** if any of you has a grievance against someone. **Forgive as the Lord forgave you.** (Colossians 3:13)*

> *Then Peter came to Jesus and asked, "Lord, how many times shall I **forgive** my brother or sister who sins against me? Up to seven times?" Jesus answered, "I tell you, not seven times, but **seventy-seven times**. (Matthew 18:21-22)*

> ***I have forgiven in the sight of Christ for your sake, <u>in order that Satan might not outwit us</u>.** For we are not unaware of his schemes. (2 Corinthians 2:10-11)*

This means that spouses are to forgive over and over so that God will forgive them and so that they don't open the door for Satan to mess with them by stirring things up even more and causing division.

These six strategies represent proactive steps that can effectively protect a marriage from attempts by the enemy to cause division. The more these become part of the norm for a couple, the less impact challenges have on them. The challenges and circumstances may not to change, but how a couple responds to them will change because the couple knows that they have the power and authority to overcome.

Applying Faith in Your Marriage

Which of these battle strategies do you need to more fully embrace? Pray, asking God to help you believe in them and act in faith to deploy them regularly.

In what ways can you deploy the battle strategies in your marriage?

Being Vigilant

---

*"Let us not become weary in doing good,
for at the proper time we will reap a harvest if we
do not give up."*
-- The Apostle Paul (Galatians 6:9)

When fighting for your marriage, you'll want to be on guard, keeping a close watch on what is happening, and discerning what's really going on in the spiritual realm. I don't mean that you need to be overly vigilant, looking for evil around every corner. But, it is important for you to be aware of the enemy's ploys and deal with them when they come up. You can be assured that you can overcome them by the authority given to you by Jesus.

Here's where I start. As I am confronted with a situation, conflict, or difficulty, I try to identify the source. I will either evaluate it, ask the Holy Spirit to reveal what's really going on, or both.

Is it a natural consequence of a choice I or someone else made?

Have I done something against God?

Is it from God? Is it part of his discipline or pruning? Is he trying to teach me or reveal something to me?

OR, Is it from the enemy?

If it is a natural consequence, I pray and ask God for wisdom about how to handle it, or sometimes simply accept it as normal. If it is a result of something I did against God, I repent and ask God to forgive me. I may also need to ask him to help me endure his punishment, discipline, or pruning. If it is from God, possibly as part of developing my character, I pray for strength to persevere. If it is from the enemy, I battle spiritually.

When I don't know for sure if it is an enemy attack, I assume it is and battle spiritually taking the approaches covered in this chapter and in the Appendices.

Close The Door To The Enemy

The enemy's goal is to cause division in marriage. He often does that by influencing our thoughts, words, or actions, so we need to guard against giving the enemy a foothold.

> *"In your anger do not sin": Do not let the sun go down while you are still angry, and* **do not give the devil a foothold.** (Ephesians 4:26-27)

I call it closing the door to the enemy. If we let negative thoughts about our spouse take hold, it will interfere with our relationship. We've opened the door. I remember a time when my wife and I were experiencing significant tension in our marriage. I didn't know where it was coming from and couldn't figure out the underlying source.

Later, I found out that she had been thinking about divorce, even though earlier in our marriage we agreed not to speak it (and she wasn't talking about it). Because she let that thought take hold, it was causing division between us. However, once she recognized what was going on after the Holy Spirit revealed it to her, she closed the door. In her mind, she said 'no' as she visualized closing the door on Satan, and she committed to work things out between us. Taking this simple action shifted the atmosphere, allowing us to talk and work though our differences. So, whenever negative thoughts about your spouse creep into your mind, reject them, and close the door!

Wield Your "Sword"

The Word of God (as written in the Bible) is the "sword of the Spirit" (Ephesians 6:17). Jesus modeled this for us. When he was tempted by the devil in the wilderness, Jesus responded with "it is written," using the Word of God to defend against the attacks.

> *The tempter came to him and said, "If you are the Son of God, tell these stones to become bread." Jesus answered, "**It is written: 'Man shall not live on bread alone, but on every word that comes from the mouth of God.**' Then the devil took him to the holy city and had him stand on the highest point of the temple. "If you are the Son of God," he said, "throw yourself down. For it is written: "'He will command his angels concerning you, and they will lift you up in their hands, so that you will not strike your foot against a stone.'" Jesus answered him, "**It is also written: 'Do not put the Lord your God to the test.**'" Again, the devil took him to a very high mountain and showed him all the kingdoms of the world and their splendor. "All this I will give you," he said, "if you will bow down and worship me." Jesus said to him, "Away from me, Satan! **For it is written: 'Worship the Lord your God, and serve him only.**'" (Matthew 4:3-10)*

In the same way, one of the ways we battle the enemy and fight for our marriage (and other areas of our life) is by declaring scripture verses that relate to the situation. For example, if I'm feeling fear, I can declare 2 Timothy 1:7 by saying: I will not bow to fear, because God's Word says (or "it is written") that "*I have not been given a spirit of fear, but of power, love, and a sound mind."* (NKJV)

If I'm feeling anxious, I can declare Philippians 4:6: I will not be anxious, for God's word says, "*Do not be anxious about anything, but in every situation, by prayer and petition, with thanksgiving, present your requests to God."* Then, I pray, give thanks to God, and the anxiety will decrease or go away, persisting until it does.

If I'm worried, I can declare Matthew 6:31-34: I don't need to worry because God's Word says "*So do not worry, saying, 'What shall we eat?' or 'What shall we drink?' or 'What shall we wear?' For the pagans run after all these things, and your heavenly Father knows that you need them. But seek first his kingdom and his righteousness, and all these things will be given to you as well. Therefore do not worry about tomorrow, for tomorrow will worry about itself. Each day has enough trouble of its own."* Then, I turn my thoughts towards God (seeking him), letting him know that I trust him to handle the situation. I persist until worry dissipates.

Recapture Ground Given Up To The Enemy

No matter how far along we are in our marriage, we all have things that control or strongly influence our thoughts, words, reactions, and behaviors in negative ways. The root is often from some type of emotional wounding we experienced earlier in life that caused us to shut down or strike out. We are also influenced by things that happened in our family of origin (mom's and dad's family tree), which the Bible calls generational iniquities. I think of them as negative or unhealthy patterns of behavior that are present in a family in multiple generations.

Strongholds are another place where ground may have been given up to the enemy. Strongholds occur when a belief or mindset becomes a routine or prominent part of how a person behaves. They are what someone relies on to defend or protect their right to believe in something. Strongholds interfere with relationships, and if not dealt with, can be a significant barrier to a healthy marriage. There is usually a spiritual root that resulted from one or more events that happened to the person earlier in life. Once the event is uncovered, Jesus can be invited in to handle the stronghold that was created. (See Appendix 2 "Overcoming Strongholds" for a list of strongholds and an approach that can be used to overcome them.)

Whenever thoughts, words, or behaviors are present that are inconsistent with God's desire for us, we have given up ground to the enemy, directly or indirectly, intentionally or unintentionally. The Holy Spirit can reveal where that has occurred so that it can be handled, usually by the individual. There may also be ground given up by the couple based on things that have happened between them during dating, engagement, or marriage.

In faith, ask *Jesus, where have I (we) given up ground to the enemy?* Listen for what is revealed. He may bring to mind a memory, person, or event. Pay attention to what you hear, see, sense, or feel. If you are unclear, ask again. Jesus is kind, loving, and merciful. He wants to set you free and he will answer. Wait expectantly with eager anticipation. Once the issues are identified, the individual or couple can handle them by repenting, forgiving, and renouncing, as led by the Holy Spirit.

Remove Undercurrents

There are many undercurrents in relationships, including unhealthy vows and agreements, lies, harsh words, and contempt. When present, these work underneath the surface to affect how we view life, ourselves, our spouse, and others. They influence how we react to situations. When we identify and remove them, our relationships become stronger and more fulfilling.

> *"Therefore, rid yourselves of all malice and all deceit, hypocrisy, envy, and slander of every kind."*
> (1 Peter 2:1)

Unhealthy vows and agreements are undercurrents, which constrain people and interfere with the marriage relationships. So, it is important to identify and break them. The enemy will persist in prompting people in their minds to knowingly or unknowingly embrace unhealthy vows and agreements, and he will try to get people to go back to them even after they are handled. [Note: vows and agreements also work against other relationships and life in general, so it is important to handle them so that increasing levels of freedom and wholeness can be experienced.]

Unhealthy vows are thoughts or statements that include never or always. They are declarations that result from a situation that occurred and are usually directly or indirectly aimed towards another person or yourself.

Examples include: I will never let her get close to me. I always mess things up. I never do it right. She will never change. He always treats me poorly. He always irritates me. We will never get over this.

Unhealthy agreements occur when we agree with (embrace) negative words or thoughts about our self (or others), or thoughts contrary to who we are in Christ, as indicated in the Bible. So, they are often some type of statement about identity. They may be the result of an interaction with another person and may be directly or indirectly about them. However, many times it is a statement that is about you, not them.

Examples include: I'm not good enough. I don't measure up. I'm depressed. I am bi-polar. I am an addict. I am crazy. I'm overwhelmed. I am a bad person/parent/spouse. I am a loser. He's a loser. She is not a good person. Our marriage is a mistake.

It's not that you don't make mistakes, or have a diagnosed condition, or exhibit unhealthy behaviors, but they don't define you. The agreement or vow takes hold and has power over us when we speak or think of it as our identity.

Past unhealthy vows and agreements must be broken to remove the undercurrent, and then any new ones that you become aware of need to be broken as soon as possible. They are broken one-by-one by giving them over to Jesus. (See Appendix 3 "Breaking Vows and Agreements" for an approach that I've used.)

Uncover and Address the Source of Overreactions

All of us have been hurt emotionally, physically, or spiritually by someone in the past, usually by someone close to us like a parent, sibling, relative, friend, co-worker, or someone in a position of authority. Some wounds are deeper than others, especially if the situation was traumatic or involved abuse of some sort.

When we react to something that happens to us today, we may be reacting the way we do because it is similar to a past situation when we were hurt emotionally, physically, or spiritually. Our reaction may have little to do with what happens in the moment. A key indicator that this is happening is when the reaction is disproportionate to the event or situation.

When an issue comes up and a spouse is triggered, it is important to uncover the root cause because it is usually not what you are seeing on the surface. In faith, simply ask, *Jesus, what's underneath this (anger, bitterness, disgust, etc.) that I'm feeling right now? What's the root of it?* Pay attention to what is revealed to you by what you hear, see, sense, or remember.

To handle what caused the trigger you may need to repent of something that you did, you may need to renounce a lie that you believed or a vow you made based on what happened, or you may need to ask Jesus or someone else for forgiveness, or you may need to forgive someone else or the situation. One spouse can be guiding the other spouse through this process, or one spouse can do this on his/her own, while the other spouse prays for the Holy Spirit to reveal what's really happening.

As an example, I tend to become defensive quickly, especially when I feel judged or criticized. When Julaine and I are working together, this can happen. We had a situation recently where I asked for and she provided feedback on a presentation that I prepared. Instead of listening to her and receiving the feedback, as she was talking, I began to defend what I developed and took offense to what I was hearing. She shut down.

In the moment, I wasn't aware of what was happening. After seeing her reaction and a little time passed, I asked the Holy Spirit to reveal to me what was going on. What I realized was that I took her feedback as criticism, as though we were not on the same team and she was telling me that I wasn't good enough or I was wrong. This reaction comes from past wounding when I was made to feel that way as a child. My pride was hurt, so I became defensive. Once I became aware of this, I repented of letting pride take hold and believing the lie that I wasn't good enough. I apologized to her for being defensive and not receiving her feedback. The distance between us didn't resolve immediately, but we did get back to normal a short time later.

Battling with each other may also take the form of joining together to ask the Holy Spirit to reveal what's going on in the situation, listening for the other spouse. Once the issue is revealed, the couple may need to take spiritual authority over it in the name of Jesus. For example, if you feel accused, take authority over it. *In the name of Jesus, I bind the spirit of accusation and command it away.* If you feel judged, take authority over it. *In the name of Jesus, I bind the spirit of judgment and command it away*. (For more examples of addressing what might be underneath overreactions, see Appendix 4 "Recognizing and Handling Spirits At Work In Marriage").

If we take the position that our spouse may be responding out of his or her wounding, we become less defensive and respond differently. When we view our spouse as a wounded person (as we all are), we can better handle his or her reactions and work though the situation. It also helps to stop and pray when an overreaction occurs or is in process.

Handle Issues When They Come Up

It is important for us to be fully tuned-in to our spouse. If you are truly interested in seeking first to understand your spouse, study him or her so that you know when something is not quite right. We are always changing, so it is important to keep observing, studying, and being curious about our spouse, desiring to know him or her better. It creates deeper intimacy when we do.

It also allows us to handle issues as they come up, rather than letting them linger and take hold. Jesus created a sense of urgency for, and priority on, handling issues between people before doing anything else.

*"Therefore, if you are offering your gift at the altar and there remember that your brother or sister has something against you, leave your gift there in front of the altar. **First go and be***

reconciled to them; then come and offer your gift. (Matthew 5:23-24)

Another way to keep tuned in to our spouse is to listen from the heart. When we listen for what's behind the words with the goal of understanding, we draw closer together and our spouse feels understood. This may help us to avoid issues, but if it doesn't, it allows us to handle them more quickly so that they are less likely to escalate.

My dear brothers and sisters, take note of this: **Everyone should be quick to listen, slow to speak and slow to become angry,** *because human anger does not produce the righteousness that God desires.* (James 1:19-20)

If issues come up, it is important to handle them quickly using some of the approaches outlined in this book, including those in the Appendices.

Applying Faith in Your Marriage

How can you be more vigilant in fighting for your marriage?

Where would it be helpful to exercise the authority of Jesus in your life and marriage?

What strongholds have been present in your life? When will you start breaking them down?

What unhealthy vows and agreements have you made? When will you break them?

AFTERWORD

God originally designed marriage between a man and woman to be a picture of oneness, an expression of the oneness between the Father, Jesus, and Holy Spirit. God desires marriage to be a lifelong covenant, just as his love for us never ends. To have a healthy marriage, it is critical for each spouse to be in a strong and growing relationship with Jesus so that he or she can be in a healthy relationship with the other spouse. When the husband and wife are whole through Jesus, their marriage will be vibrant and thrive.

The first marriage between Adam and Eve came under attack, taking what was "very good" and introducing blame, shame, pain, strife, discord, division, and a whole host of things interfering with oneness. So, why should it be a surprise that Christian marriages today are under attack?

I believe that a marriage, especially a Christian marriage, without an active faith and growing relationship with Jesus at the center, is unprotected against attack by the spiritual forces of wickedness. The divorce rate among Christians may be an indicator that Christ is not fully at the center of the marriage.

Jesus died for our sins so that we could have a direct relationship with God. His shed blood cleanses us and protects us. By rising from the dead, Jesus overcame Satan and took authority back. Jesus, in turn, gave authority in his name to us so that we can overcome Satan because he still rules this world and will until Jesus comes again.

Our only protection is Jesus. When we put on the armor of God, we are putting on the fullness of Jesus, completely equipped for the spiritual war that we are in for our life and marriage. The enemy can't stand against a marriage when both the husband and wife have an active and growing relationship with Jesus – living consistent with biblical principles, praying together, and battling together for their marriage.

Are you convinced?

If not, what will it take to convince you of the importance of living your life and marriage with Jesus at the center? I urge you to continue to explore it until you find the answers you are seeking.

It is all about faith, believing in what you can't see. However, as you place your faith in Jesus and develop a growing relationship with him, you will get to experience a fulfilling life and marriage. It's not necessarily going to be easy, but it will be rewarding -- better than you ever dreamed. And, you will have all you need to overcome any challenge that comes your way.

You may be finding it difficult to believe that putting Jesus at the center of your life and marriage will make a difference. You may even feel like you have been doing that to no avail. I urge you to persevere. If your heart is truly with Jesus and you have an active relationship with him, believing fully that he will do all that he promises, your marriage can be healthy and well. When you stand on the covenant that you made when you said your wedding vows and stand firmly on your faith in Jesus, you will see victory! It may take time, and it may not look like you imagine, but keep your faith in marriage with Jesus at the center and see what happens.

If you are in a struggling marriage right now and feel like you have tried everything else, why not give Jesus a chance? What have you got to lose? If your marriage is dead, will you give Jesus the opportunity to resurrect it? Think that's not possible? As you've read my story, you know that it is not only possible, but that it happens. Miracles are possible when you open yourself up to Jesus and allow him to work in and through you.

If your marriage is in a good place right now, consider how it might be better, stronger, and healthier with Jesus at the center. Consider how you may be able to overcome challenges more quickly and effectively. Consider how your life may be richer, fuller. I invite you to explore the possibilities by putting to action some of the new things you read in this book.

If your faith in and relationship with Jesus is strong and you are already applying biblical principles to your marriage regularly, thank God for blessing you and letting your marriage be an example for others. I hope you found one or two things from this book that you hadn't considered before, and that you will start applying them in your life and marriage.

May your faith in marriage, living with Jesus at the center, give you the strength to persevere, overcome, and thrive. And, may God bless, strengthen, and protect your marriage.

Appendices

Appendix 1: Enemy Arrows and Kingdom Weapons

So I say, walk by the Spirit, and you will not gratify
the desires of the flesh. For the flesh desires what is
contrary to the Spirit, and the Spirit what is contrary
to the flesh. They are in conflict with each other, so
that you are not to do whatever you want.
-- The Apostle Paul (Galatians 5:16-17)

Enemy Arrows

The enemy has many ways ("desires of the flesh") of interfering with our relationship with God and our spouse, so I call these the enemy arrows. They keep us from experiencing the fullness of God in our life because they harm ourselves or others. In most cases, they have to do with keeping us engaged in unhealthy behaviors or attitudes, including:

Unloving	Unnatural sex	Stealing
Hatred	Orgies	Coveting
Jealousy	Idolatry, Witchcraft	Lying (falsehood)
Bitterness	Factions	Provoking
Conceit	Discord (variance)	Obscenity
Lust, Envy, Greed	Fits of rage (anger)	Unwholesome talk
Evil desires	Dissensions (strife)	Foolish talk
Selfish ambition	Debauchery	Coarse joking
Insolent	Drunkenness	Hypocrisy
Proud	Wickedness	Lacking self-control
Arrogant, Boastful	Depravity	Brawling, Brutal
Ungrateful	Murder	Abusive, Rash
Unholy	Deceit, Malice	Treacherous
Unforgiving	Gossip, Slander	Love themselves
Impurity	Hating God	Love money
Infidelity	Disobeying parents	Love pleasure
Sexual immorality	Being unmerciful	

Source: Galatians 5:19-21, 26, Romans 1:26-32, Romans 13:8-14, Ephesians 4:25-32, 5:1-20, Colossians 3:5-11, 2 Timothy 3:1-5, 1 Peter 2:1-3

If any of these are present in your life, take steps to remove them. Get help if needed. If we want to be in close relationship with Jesus, we need to avoid these. Otherwise, they interfere with the flow of the Holy Spirit and give the devil a foothold that he will use to separate us from God and from our spouse.

Kingdom Weapons

We overcome many of these ploys from the enemy by *choosing* behaviors and attitudes that align with God, which I call Kingdom Weapons, including:

Love	Rejoice	Overcome evil with
Joy	Mourn with mourning	good
Peace	Live in harmony	Not self-seeking
Forbearance/patience	Live at peace	Not easily angered
Kindness	Rejoice with the truth	Keep no record of
Goodness	Protect	wrongs
Faithfulness	Trust	Do what is right
Gentleness	Hope	Do not curse
Self-control	Persevere	Do not be proud
Hope	Have faith	Do not be conceited
Joyful in hope	Speak truthfully	Do not take revenge
Patient in affliction	Build others up	Do not envy
Faithful in prayer	Be compassionate	Do not boast
Devoted to one	Be forgiving	Do not dishonor
another	Be righteousness	others
Honor one another	Be truthful	Do not delight in
Help people in need	Give thanks	evil
Practice hospitality	Act in humility	
Bless persecutors	Show gratitude	

Source: Galatians 5:22-26, Romans 5:1-5, Romans 12:9-21, 1 Corinthians 13, Ephesians 4:25-32, 5:1-20, Colossians 3:12-17

When these weapons are embraced and lived out routinely, the enemy's arrows no longer penetrate, and we experience freedom and relational health.

Appendix 2: Overcoming Strongholds

"The weapons we fight with are not the weapons of the world. On the contrary, they have divine power to demolish strongholds."
-- The Apostle Paul (2 Corinthians 10:4)

Strongholds are mental fortresses that hinder a person's ability to walk freely in the spirit and are very dangerous. Their aim is to strangle the Word out of people and control their speech, behavior, and thoughts. (Source: Original Design International)

Identifying Strongholds

The following list includes some of the more common strongholds that people experience.
(Source: Freedom Coach Training, Oaks Rising)

Suspicion: Being painfully deceived can cause the building of a stronghold of suspicion to protect against being deceived again. This stronghold will resist intimacy with God.

Doubt: This is usually one of the most obvious strongholds. It frequently accompanies a stronghold of suspicion which can masquerade so well, its existence is often totally denied.

Independence: Rejection can cause the building of a stronghold of independence and self-sufficiency around pain, fortifying a right to never be vulnerable again. This can include any vulnerability to the work of the Holy Spirit.

False Security: When unmet needs exist, a stronghold of false security may be erected. The stronghold projects a façade of great strength intended to keep others from knowing how internally fragile and needy a person is. This can extend to keeping God at arm's length, as well.

Confusion: Is erected by the old nature to mask the true understanding of a given issue or many issues. This stronghold leads to discouragement and depression (which can be strongholds, too).

Unforgiveness: When someone has been abused or deeply hurt, unless forgiveness and healing come, strongholds of unforgiveness, bitterness, or anger are erected to justify the role of being a victim.

Distrust: Betrayal can cause the building of a stronghold of distrust to prevent anyone from getting close enough to betray again. This person will generally also be unable to fully trust God whose perfect love casts out fear.

Control and Manipulation: A childhood filled with chaos, instability and everything seemingly out of control can build a stronghold of control to prevent ever being at the mercy of another again.

Self-Indulgence: Built to justify and protect the right to indulge self to compensate for unmet needs and pain. It also justifies a right to chemically alter reality with drugs and alcohol to blot out pain.

Fear: Fear is a common, but slightly different stronghold. People generally do not build this stronghold for protection, rather it is erected around great apprehension and anxiety over unresolved experiences and memories.

Denial: A stronghold of denial refuses to acknowledge any of the above things. Denial is a valid, temporary mental and emotional coping mechanism to enable the human mind to survive certain traumatic situations similar to how shock shuts down and prevents a severely wounded body from death. Denial enables abused children to survive unbearable situations. Just as shock becomes dangerous and life-threatening when a person cannot come out of it, so does denial when it becomes a stronghold.

Handling Strongholds

Once you recognize and become aware of a stronghold in your life, in order to walk in freedom, you'll need to handle it by renouncing it, repenting of having partnered with it, and taking authority over it to cast it out of your life. It might look like this:

- ❖ Identify the stronghold (ask the Holy Spirit to reveal it to you)
- ❖ Reject the hold that it had on you
- ❖ Bind the stronghold in the name of Jesus
- ❖ Renounce the lie associated with it
- ❖ Replace the lie with truth
- ❖ Receive the truth and seal the exchange

For example, let's say pride has been a stronghold in your life. Here's how you might get rid of it, after you've submitted yourself to God. (Remember James 4:17. Submit to God, then resist the devil.) You can say something as simple as, *I choose to submit myself completely to you, Jesus.*

I recognize that I have been controlled by pride and it has become a stronghold in my life. I now reject the hold that pride has had on my life and I bind the stronghold of pride in the name of Jesus and loose it from my life. I renounce the lies that I know what's best and that I am always right. I nail these lies to the cross and give them to Jesus. The truth is that God is the only one who knows what's best and is always right. My ways are not His ways (Isaiah 55:8) and He works all things for the good of those who love Him (Romans 8:28), and I do love Him. I receive this truth in exchange for the lies I believed from the stronghold of pride and I receive that pride no longer has a hold on me, sealing it in the name of the Father, Son, and Holy Spirit. Father, fill the space that used to be occupied by pride with your love and humility.

You may need to do this more than once before the stronghold breaks completely and no longer controls you because it has had a tight grip on you for a long time. If you don't feel released from the stronghold, persist. It is called a stronghold because it is holding on strongly! It is deeply rooted. You may also benefit from the help of someone who is trained to guide people to break free from strongholds, or a Holy Spirit led Christian counselor.

To remain in freedom, you will need to take care to avoid partnering with (embracing) anything that could be related to the stronghold so that it doesn't take hold again.

Appendix 3: Breaking Unhealthy Vows and Agreements

Unhealthy vows and agreements are undercurrents working against the health of marriage, which are used by the enemy to constrain people and to interfere with relationships. So, it is important to identify and break them. I've found it is best to address each vow or agreement separately, rather than trying to handle a group of them. Here's an approach that's worked for me:

- ❖ Identify the unhealthy vow or agreement (ask the Holy Spirit to reveal it if you can't identify it on your own)
- ❖ Reject the vow or agreement
- ❖ Renounce the lie associated with the vow or agreement
- ❖ Replace the lie with truth
- ❖ Seal the work

Here's how you might get rid of it, after you've submitted yourself to God. (Remember James 4:17. Submit to God, then resist the devil.) You can say something as simple as, *I give myself entirely to you, Jesus.*

Holy Spirit, fill me afresh and heighten my senses to be aware of how you are communicating with me. Where have I made vows and agreements? (Let's say he reveals that you've vowed not to get close to your wife and believed that she doesn't care about you.) *I reject and renounce the vow I made that I will never get close to my wife. I repent of agreeing with the lie that she doesn't care about me. Jesus, please forgive me for making this vow and agreeing with this lie. I nail to the cross the lie that she doesn't care about me. The truth is that you brought us together and you have made her to care about me. She does care about me and has shown it in many ways. Jesus, I receive the truth that my wife cares deeply about me to replace the lie that she doesn't care. I seal it in the name of the Father, Son, and Holy Spirit. What's been done here cannot be undone. It is complete.*

Be aware that things may happen that will make you doubt whether the unhealthy vow or agreement has been broken. Don't take the bait! If that happens, simply reject the vow or agreement and state that you have already handled it. If you pick it up again, you'll be back where you started. Walking in freedom will take diligence on your part so that you don't believe the lies again.

Appendix 4: Recognizing and Handling Spirits at Work in Marriage

When we acknowledge that our battle is not against flesh and blood (not against our spouse), but against things in the spiritual realm, it is important that we quickly recognize and handle spirits at work so that they don't take hold and cause conflict or other problems.

Identifying Spirits at Work

Many of the spirits that work against us are familiar and even commonly used terms, often associated with a feeling we are experiencing. When you think about it, all of them go against God, his nature, or his desire for us. Foul, unclean, and evil spirits at work include:

abandonment	discouragement	negativity
accusation	division	perfectionism
addiction	dread, doubt	pride
adultery	envy	pornography
affliction	fear	poverty, rejection
anger, anxiety	gossip	religion
argumentation	guilt	self-centeredness
bitterness	hatred	self-harm
bullying	hopelessness	self-righteousness
confusion	infidelity	sickness
contempt	infirmity	shame
condemnation	jealousy	stress
control, criticism	judgment	stubbornness
cynicism	lies	suicide
deception	lust	torment
depression	manipulation	unbelief
despair	oppression	unforgiveness

How do you know that any of these spirits are at work? Pay attention to how you feel or what you are experiencing at any given time. If you feel a sudden shift in the atmosphere or mood, chances are that a foul spirit is present.

For example, one day my wife and I were having a conversation. Things were going well until she said something to me and I suddenly felt accused. I could feel my temperature start to rise and I started to get defensive. However, I recognized that something had changed, so I asked her if we could stop and take authority over the situation. Then, I simply said, *In the name of Jesus, I command the spirit of accusation away.* That simple act diffused the situation and allowed us to continue the conversation instead of it escalating into an argument.

Handling Spirits

Jesus has won! So, we don't need to let these spirits bully, torment, or bother us. We simply need to take authority over them. Speak out loud (even if a whisper) something like this: *In the name of Jesus Christ, I command the spirit of [name the spirit at work] to be bound in chains and I send you to Jesus. I am a child of God and you have no place here.*

Once you do this, you should sense a positive shift in the atmosphere or situation. If not, persist by repeating your command in the authority of Jesus until the situation improves. If it doesn't, ask the Holy Spirit to reveal if another spirit is at work. *Holy Spirit, if there is another spirit at work, reveal it to me now.* Listen, then take authority (by repeating the command above) over whatever word comes into your mind. Assume what you hear is from the Holy Spirit if it is something that is not consistent with

God's nature, what his desire would be for you, or God's Word as recorded in the Bible.

Overcoming When Triggered

Whenever we are triggered by our spouse (or anyone else), a good default position is that we are not struggling against the other person, but we are battling against unseen forces trying to cause division and break the relationship (Ephesians 6:12). When we believe that to be the case, we need to battle differently, using spiritual weapons, primarily standing on the Word of God as written in the Bible and taking authority in the name of Jesus as we are instructed to in the Bible.

I've come to believe that conflict in marriage almost always has a spiritual underpinning. A primary goal of the enemy is to cause division, particularly between a husband and wife. So, when an issue causes significant tension in my marriage, my first response usually is dealing with the spiritual realm. Or, if I've tried to reconcile differences using usual conflict resolution approaches and they haven't worked, then I see if I can address the issue spiritually.

Here are some considerations:

- ❖ **Handle the issue quickly!** Do not let it take root.
- ❖ **Identify the spirit at work** – Accusation? Judgment? Criticism? Anger? Something else? (This is usually what you or your spouse is feeling in the moment.)
- ❖ **Take authority over the spirit and cast it out.** For example: *In the name of Jesus Christ, I bind the spirit of* (name it) *and I separate it from myself and* (spouse name), *and I send it to Jesus for judgment.*

- ❖ **Forgive, repent, and/or renounce** something, if appropriate.
- ❖ **Love your spouse through it.** One thing to try is to hug each other for at least 30 seconds, even if you don't want to.
- ❖ **Remove all variance**, whether spoken or only in thought, so that the Spirit can once again flow freely.
- ❖ **Pray.** Invite Jesus into the situation. Ask the Holy Spirit to reveal what's really going on, the root of the issue, possibly the wound that was opened causing the reaction
- ❖ **Stand on the Word of God.** Speak truth (Scripture) to overcome the lies and to diffuse the situation. Identify a scripture passage that fits the situation and declare it by speaking it out loud. Repeat when necessary until the atmosphere shifts back to peace.

If you are in a location or an emotional state that won't allow for you to take the above steps, then agree with each other to come back to it later. Then, ask Jesus to put what you are feeling in a safe place. *Jesus, we ask you to put in a safe place all of these emotions and everything that is going on here and between us until we have time to handle it. Amen.* Come back to it at a later time when you are in a better position to address it using the steps above.

ABOUT THE AUTHOR

AFTER A 30-YEAR career in marketing, Doug Bierl turned his attention towards helping to build, restore, and strengthen healthy marriages through professional coaching, training, and writing.

Doug married during college and had four children within seven years. He poured most of his time and energy into advancing in his education and career, largely at the expense of his marriage and family. He didn't invest time in his marriage relationship and drifted apart from his wife. So, fifteen years into the marriage, he decided to end it, not wanting to address the underlying reasons or do the work needed to restore the marriage.

A year after his divorce, Doug met Julaine, whom he married six months later. She was divorced, with two children and so Doug and Julaine blended a family of six children between the ages of 5 and 16. Through the years they experienced many ups and downs (and still do). Doug and Julaine are happily married and they have learned a lot from their experience, including the importance of investing in the health of their marriage, even and especially when things are going well. They are intentional about focusing on their marriage and making it a high priority in their life.

Doug and Julaine now use their experience, as well as approaches they've been trained and certified in, to work as "Marriage Navigators" journeying with engaged and married couples to help navigate the ups and downs of marriage. They also conduct marriage wellness workshops to provide couples with tools to help keep their marriage healthy. Their heart is for helping to keep marriages healthy and strong.

Doug has written another book, *The Divorce Pill*, to give couples a glimpse into what divorce could look like. The intent is that, after reading the book, the couple will be more fully informed to decide whether addressing their challenges would be better for them than divorcing. He hopes they will choose to stay married to each other.

You can learn more at www.ReclaimingWholeness.Life.

www.ingramcontent.com/pod-product-compliance
Lightning Source LLC
LaVergne TN
LVHW021505080426
835509LV00018B/2411